SEAFOOD

BARBECUE & GRILL

SEAFOOD
BARBECUE & GRILL

with **PETER HOWARD**

NEW HOLLAND

First published in Australia in 2010 by
New Holland Publishers (Australia) Pty Ltd
Sydney • Auckland • London • Cape Town

www.newholland.com.au

1/66 Gibbes Street Chatswood NSW 2067 Australia
218 Lake Road Northcote Auckland New Zealand
86 Edgware Road London W2 2EA United Kingdom
80 McKenzie Street Cape Town 8001 South Africa

A record of this book is available at the National Library of Australia:

ISBN 9781742570136.

Publisher: Fiona Schultz
Publishing manager: Lliane Clarke
Project editor: Talina McKenzie
Photography: R&R PhotoStudio, Sydney Fish Market, Michael McGrath, Graeme Gillies, Joe Filshie
Designer: Emma Gough
Cover design: Emma Gough
Production manager: Olga Dementiev
Printer: Toppan Leefung Printing Limited (China)

ACKNOWLEDGEMENTS

Kinkawooka Shellfish Co for
the most delicious mussels,
which are already de-bearded
and scrubbed, and for the
Boston Bay clams, which are
succulent and sweet.

CONTENTS

STARTERS

SALADS

MAINS

PETER'S FOREWORD

If I had a dollar for each time I've been asked about cooking seafood on a barbecue, I'd be sitting in some exotic resort sipping some exotic cocktail with never a thought about earning a dollar ever again! But I didn't get the dollar each time I was asked and so the next best thing for me to do is to write about barbecuing seafood.

Writing and cooking are two of my all time favourite occupations! I must admit I used to be intimidated with cooking seafood and through many years of cooking I have come to recognise that the same principles apply to cooking these delicious morsels from the deep blue sea and aquaculture on the barbecue applies as it does to regular cooking.

Choosing your seafood to do what is required of it is ultimately the most important rule. I asked Roberta Muir from the Sydney Fish Market's Seafood School to put together some points to look for when you're purchasing and storing your seafood. Who would know better, as this is a fabulous school with a huge following of locals and increasingly, international guests?

Delicate flesh needs a little TLC on the barbecue, just as it does in a pan or in an oven. More sympathetic and subtle additives are required to bring out the flavour of the seafood and not drown it; spicy dishes require a bigger flavoured fish to take the heftier flavours without overwhelming the naturally beautiful flavours. I don't want to say it is commonsense, because if it were this book would not be necessary.

However, a lot of it comes down to knowing your seafood—so I have put as much information as possible into the recipes and made points about cooking seafood in each recipe so it is more immediate… it's there on the page with you at the barbecue or in the kitchen.

Tasmania is blessed with a pristine environment in which seafood is produced—what a glorious place our Island State is. In the past I have had the honour of cooking some of their seafood in America during the G'day LA and G'day USA promotional campaigns. The Americans love it and what's not to love as it tastes—yes really tastes as seafood should.

I have used fish and other seafood items that are not on the endangered species list—we must all be aware of the issue that we can quite easily fish our ocean out of this amazing resource we call fresh Australian seafood. For this advice, I have relied on the Maritime Stewardship Council and Duncan Leadbitter, the Director Asia Pacific Marine Stewardship Council (MSC).

SEAFOOD PURCHASING TIPS

SUSTAINABLE SEAFOOD

Make the best environmental choice when buying seafood.

Many of the fish we are accustomed to eating are in danger of disappearing altogether through overfishing. It is our responsibility to ensure sufficient wild fish remain in the oceans for all future generations to enjoy.

Consumers should look for the distinctive blue oval, Marine Stewardship Council (MSC) eco-label. Seafood bearing this label has been certified as sustainably harvested (see below).

If the fish you want does not have this label, ask your fishmonger why not and suggest they only stock MSC certified products.

A copy of Australia's Sustainable Seafood Guide can be obtained from the Australian Marine Conservation Society at: www.amcs.org.au.

THE MARINE STEWARDSHIP COUNCIL (MSC)

Ensuring that there will always be plenty more fish in the sea.

Over the past 30 years, areas of the oceans that are classified as overfished have tripled. Today one in four fisheries are regarded as overfished. A global study released by an international group of ecologists and economists in November 2006 indicated that there will not be sufficient wild seafood left in the oceans by 2048. With fish numbers around the world declining at an alarming rate, this is the issue that is shaping our thinking in the 21st century.

A growing interest in the state of fisheries—and the value of certification as a tool to drive sustainable fishing—resulted in the establishment of the Marine Stewardship Council (MSC) in 1997.

The MSC is a non-profit international body whose role is to identify—via a stringent certification program—well-managed fisheries in order to help wholesalers, retailers and consumers make the right choice when buying seafood.

Consumers should look for the distinctive blue oval, Marine Stewardship Council eco-label. Seafood bearing this label has been certified as sustainably harvested.

Australian consumers can play a powerful role in ensuring that future generations will enjoy the delightful range of seafood that Australians have long taken for granted by becoming aware of and questioning how their seafood is sourced. The MSC is becoming the name associated with a global solution to this problem through its environmental standards for well-managed and sustainable fisheries.

Some of the world's most important retailers embrace the philosophy of sustainable fishing and commit to sourcing their supply of seafood from fisheries that meet the MSC's independent environmental standard. MSC eco-labelled products, with their easily recognisable MSC blue oval logo, are now on sale in 26 countries, including Australia.

The MSC is increasingly being recognised by industry, endorsed by conservationists, respected by scientists and preferred by consumers. With its Asia Pacific office based in Australia, the MSC aims to promote its unique approach to driving sustainable fishing to industry and consumers alike.

Concerned and discerning consumers can make a substantial and ongoing contribution to the vital task of meeting the seafood needs of the present without compromising the needs of the future.

PURCHASING TIPS FROM SYDNEY SEAFOOD SCHOOL

There is little doubt that the Sydney Seafood School at Sydney Fish Market is THE authority when it comes to knowing all about seafood. I asked my lovely friend, Roberta Muir, Manager of the Sydney Seafood School, to give us some tips on what to look for when buying and storing seafood for your barbecue meal. Thanks Roberta!

WHAT TO LOOK FOR WHEN BUYING SEAFOOD:

Whole fish

- Bright and lustrous skin or scales.
- Firm flesh that springs back when touched.
- Bright pink-red gills.
- Pleasant, fresh sea smell.

Fillets and cutlets

- Bright, lustrous and firm flesh.
- Any dark muscle should be a pink-red colour.
- Pleasant, fresh sea smell.
- No discolouration, gaping wounds or bruising.

Crustaceans and molluscs

- Brightly coloured, lustrous shells or flesh.
- Firm and intact shells, heads, tentacles or flesh.
- Shells closed or close when tapped or gently squeezed.
- Pleasant, fresh sea smell.
- No discolouration, particularly at joints.

Seafood will stay fresh longer if it's kept cold. When shopping for fresh seafood use a chiller bag/esky or ask your fishmonger to pack some ice with your purchase.

SEAFOOD STORAGE TIPS

REFRIGERATING

- Scale, clean, gut and rinse fish, squid, cuttlefish and octopus, place in a plastic bag on a plate or tray or in a covered container.
- Use within 2–3 days.
- Dead crustaceans (such as prawns) should be consumed as soon as possible after purchase. Refrigerate in a plastic bag on a plate or tray or in a covered container.
- Live crustaceans (such as crabs) and molluscs (such as mussels) should be consumed as soon as possible after purchase. Place in a container, cover with damp butchers' paper and keep in the warmest part of the refrigerator, which is usually the crisper (optimum 5°C).

FREEZING

- Whole non-oily fish can be frozen for up to 6 months at -18°C or less (many domestic freezers do not get this cold, if in doubt, check).
- Whole oily fish, fillets, cutlets, crustaceans (such as lobsters, prawns, crabs) and molluscs (such as mussels, abalone, squid) can be frozen for up to 3 months at -18°C or less.

FISH

- Scale, gut, gill and rinse all fish before freezing.
- Place in an airtight freezer bag, label, date and freeze as above.

CRUSTACEANS (EXCEPT PRAWNS) AND MOLLUSCS

- Gut and clean squid, cuttlefish and octopus before freezing.
- Place in an airtight freezer bag or container, label, date and freeze as above.

PRAWNS

- Place unpeeled prawns in a plastic container appropriate to the volume of prawns. Cover with water, seal and freeze. This forms a large iceblock, which insulates the prawns. Do not add salt as it draws out the moisture.
- Label, date and freeze as above.

You can find more information on seafood purchase and storage, seafood recipes, species information and answers to frequently asked questions on the FISHline pages of Sydney Fish Market's website: www.sydneyfishmarket.com.au.

The full program of Sydney Seafood School classes is also on the website and you can request a copy of the program or subscribe to the regular FISHline Newsletter by emailing fishline@sydneyfishmarket.com.au or calling 02 9004 1122.

STAR

TERS

GETTING A BARBECUE OFF TO A GOOD START IS CRUCIAL — IT INVOLVES BEING ORGANISED AND KNOWING WHAT IS GOING TO HAPPEN ... THEN MAKING IT SEEM LIKE IT IS ALL GOING ALONG WITHOUT ORGANISATION!

IT'S A KNACK!

COOKING AND EATING AROUND THE BARBECUE INVOLVES EVERYONE AND THAT'S GOOD, BUT THERE ARE TIMES WHEN YOU NEED A LITTLE BIT MORE FORMALITY AND SIT-DOWN DISHES ARE REQUIRED TOO.

ALL THOSE RECIPE REQUIREMENTS ARE HERE FOR YOU ... READ ON!

MANDARIN VODKA CHERVIL OYSTERS

SERVES 4

24 Pacific oysters, freshly shucked

30–40ml mandarin vodka

6–8 mandarin segments, drained from can and cut into small pieces

chervil sprigs

rock salt for serving

Ensure the oysters are clear of visible shell grit. Take them to the barbecue with the vodka. Put them on a hot open grill and spoon some vodka over the oysters—do not overfill them because the vodka will ignite if it spills over the edge. Do only 6–8 oysters at a time.

They are ready to go when there is a little bubbling around the edge of the oyster flesh—do NOT overcook!

Remove from the barbecue, top with a piece of mandarin segment and some chervil sprigs—serve on a cocktail napkin, around the barbecue, while warm.

ANGELS ON HORSEBACK

SERVES 4

16 large oysters out of shell

16 pieces of bacon, rindless, 8cm long x 3cm wide (3in x1in)

toothpicks

Worcestershire sauce

Wrap each oyster in a piece of bacon and secure with a toothpick.

Spray a hot plate with a little oil and cook the angels at high temperature until bacon is crisp. Brush a little Worcestershire sauce onto the oysters as they cook.

Serve the angels on suitable plate with a little Worcestershire sauce on the side—these are great served around the barbie as guests arrive.

SEMILLON SAUVIGNON BLANC
OYSTERS

SERVES 4

48 freshly-shucked oysters, on the shell

250ml semillon sauvignon blanc wine

2 tablespoons chives, chopped

1 teaspoon pink peppercorns, rinsed and roughly crushed

250g salted butter, in 2cm cubes

Check the oysters are grit free—try not to rinse under running water as you lose that lovely saltwater flavour of freshly shucked oysters.

Boil the wine and simmer for 2 minutes. Add the chives and peppercorns and simmer for a minute. Remove from the heat and swirl in the butter to melt and combine.

Put the oysters onto the open grill about 8 at a time, spoon over some of the sauce. When the liquid is bubbling, the oysters are ready to serve.

Carefully place the oysters onto heaped rock salt on a platter to keep the oysters upright or onto finely shredded, outer lettuce leaves for the same reason. Leave to cool so they can be picked up and slipped out of the shell and into your mouth.

This wine sauce is similar to a beurre blanc and you can use it on barbecued white fish. Add citrus to it if you like.

OYSTERS IN PROSCIUTTO

SERVES 4

24 freshly shucked oysters, out of shell

24 x 10cm long slices prosciutto

toothpicks

olive oil spray

2 lemon cheeks

Wrap each oyster loosely in a piece of prosciutto and secure with a toothpick.

Spray the flat plate with a little oil and cook on medium temperature flat plate until crisp, around 2–3 minutes.

Put onto platter, squeeze with lemon and pass round as you barbecue.

CHARDONNAY BUTTER OYSTERS

SERVES 4

48 opened oysters, on the shell

1 cup chardonnay wine

2 green spring onions

1 teaspoon ground black pepper

200g (7oz) unsalted butter

chopped parsley

Pour the wine into a saucepan and bring to the boil. Meanwhile, trim and finely mince the spring onions. Add to wine and simmer for 2 minutes. Remove from the heat and dice in the butter and swirl to let the butter melt and combine with the wine.

Put the oysters on a hot grill about 6 to 8 at a time. Spoon on some of the butter and sprinkle over the chopped parsley. The liquid around the edge of each oyster needs to be just bubbling to indicate the oysters are ready to serve. Do not boil or overcook as they shrink easily.

These are best served around the barbecue. Lift onto a plate filled with rock salt to 'secure' them. To eat, slip out of the shell and into your mouth and have a container to take the empty shells.

If you have any butter left over, it will store and can be used over fish or chicken at any time. Reheat in a saucepan or microwave.

OYSTERS WITH GARLIC OIL AND PRESERVED LEMON

SERVES 4

24 large Coffin Bay oysters or Sydney Rock oysters, freshly shucked

garlic oil

rock salt

preserved lemon rind to taste, washed and minced or very finely sliced

cracked black pepper

Place the oysters onto a hot grill and drizzle with a little garlic oil. Cook for 1–2 minutes. The rim of the oyster flesh should start to bubble, which indicates the oysters are ready to serve.

Serve the oysters on a bed of rock salt (to stop them slipping) on individual plates. Top with preserved lemon and sprinkle with cracked pepper. Be mindful that the shells are very hot to handle and will continue cooking for a couple of minutes after they have been removed from the heat.

Preserved lemon can be very strong in flavour so use sparingly.

OYSTERS AND CAFÉ DE PARIS BUTTER

SERVES 4

24 Pacific oysters, freshly shucked

6 x 1cm-thick slices of Café de Paris butter, cut into quarters (see page 36)

rock salt for serving

4 lemon cheeks

Sit oysters on a medium–hot open grill—ensure they sit as upright as possible. Put a quarter piece of butter on top of each one. Drop the lid and cook until the sides of the oysters are just bubbling and butter melting.

Meanwhile, heap the salt onto individual dinner plates. Lift the oysters from the grill and sit firmly into the salt so they sit upright. Serve with a lemon cheek.

CAFÉ DE PARIS BUTTER

250g unsalted butter, room temperature

1 teaspoon capers, rinsed

1 clove garlic, roughly chopped

1 tablespoon tomato paste

1 tablespoon smooth French mustard

1 teaspoon parsley, chopped

1 teaspoon tarragon leaves, chopped

¼ teaspoon paprika

1 anchovy fillet, drained

1 tablespoon lemon juice

1 teaspoon green peppercorns

Put all the ingredients into a food processor and process until smooth. Lift out onto a large piece of plastic wrap and shape into a sausage/log. Roll and secure the ends—chill to set or freeze. Slice when needed, directly from the freezer with a warmed knife.

CHARGRILLED BABY OCTOPUS WITH MANGO SALSA

SERVES 4

20 baby octopus, cleaned and tenderised

2 tablespoons vegetable oil

1/4 teaspoon sea salt

MANGO SALSA

500g mango flesh, diced into 1cm cubes

100g Spanish onion, finely diced

1 large green fruity chilli, deseeded and finely chopped

2 tablespoons orange juice

1 tablespoon orange zest, finely grated

Put the octopus in with the oil and salt, toss then let sit for 10 minutes. This eliminates the need to oil the barbecue plate when cooking.

Mix the mango, onion, chilli, juice and zest. Sit for 10 minutes.

Cook the octopus over high heat on the flat plate. Toss to cook them evenly. The trick is to not overcook them as they go tough—once firm they are ready to go.

Put the salsa into the middle of a large plate and place the octopus around it.

Serve with a good green salad if you want a more substantial starter.

BLACK MUSSELS WITH GARLIC AND RED WINE BUTTER

SERVES 4

24 black mussels, cleaned and beards removed

1 cup garlic and red wine butter (see page 40)

fresh bread, a baguette or ciabiatta

Put the mussels onto a medium-hot open grill plate. Very shortly they will start to open—lift each one into a bowl as they do. When all are removed and cool enough to handle, discard the empty top shell from each mussel. Dot each mussel with some butter (don't overload as the butter will melt and spill onto the flames). Put back onto the open grill and lower the hood for 1 minute—mussels are cooked when bubbling and the butter has melted.

Serve on individual plates with melted garlic and red wine butter if you like and plenty of good bread for dunking into the juices.

Black mussels must be fresh. You can tell by tipping them into a sinkful of water—discard any floaters. They can take a long time to clean—scrubbing and removing the beard, which it anchors itself with in the sea. Kinkawooka brand mussels, however, have done that for you and are in good fish shops now.

GARLIC AND RED WINE BUTTER

250g salted butter, room temperature

4 cloves garlic, roughly chopped

2 tablespoons parsley, roughly chopped

3 tablespoons red wine

½ tablespoon black pepper, freshly ground

Combine all ingredients in a processor or by whipping with a fork or whisk. This will keep, if you don't use it all, in an airtight container.

PRAWN KEBABS WITH PINEAPPLE CORIANDER SALSA

SERVES 4

16 green king prawns, peeled completely and de-veined

3 tablespoons pineapple juice

1 tablespoon vegetable oil

1 teaspoon Thai green curry paste

4 stainless steel skewers

vegetable oil spray

PINEAPPLE CORIANDER SALSA

60g white onion, roughly chopped

150g pineapple, peeled and roughly chopped

1 small red chilli (flesh only), chopped

1 cup coriander leaves, loosely packed

Toss the prawns with the juice, oil and curry paste—let sit for 15 minutes. Thread the prawns onto the skewers so you have four on each one. This is best done by curling the prawns in their natural form and then pushing the skewer through.

Spray with oil and cook on medium–hot flat plate for 1 minute; spray with oil and turn again and cook through—baste with the pineapple marinade at least once.

Put all salsa ingredients into a food processor and work to a runny paste. This salsa is quite runny and it is best served immediately.

Serve on large platter with pineapple salsa spooned over the top.

KAFFIR LIME PRAWNS WITH SWEET CHILLI SAUCE

SERVES 4

20 green king pawns, peeled and de-veined, tails on

2 kaffir lime leaves, ribs removed and finely shredded

1 lime, juiced

2 tablespoons peanut oil

sweet chilli sauce (see page 43)

coriander leaves, for decoration

Marinate the prawns in a small bowl containing the shredded leaves, lime juice and oil for 20 minutes.

Drain the prawns, toss onto a hot flat plate and move around to cook through.

Pour some chilli sauce into a bowl for dipping and place in the centre of a large plate—put the prawns around the bowl and decorate with the coriander leaves.

SWEET CHILLI SAUCE

MAKES 2–3 CUPS APPROXIMATELY

5 long red chillies, deseeded and roughly chopped

2 coriander roots, washed, trimmed and roughly chopped

3 garlic cloves, roughly chopped

1 teaspoon fish sauce

1 cup coconut vinegar

1 cup palm sugar, roughly grated

Pulse the chillies, coriander roots, garlic and fish sauce to a fine pulp in a food processor.

Pour the chilli mixture into a small saucepan with the vinegar and sugar—boil then simmer for 15 minutes until thickened. Cool.

What you don't use will keep in the refrigerator for at least 7 days.

PESTO-INFUSED PRAWN SKEWERS

SERVES 4

16 green king prawns (look for Spencer Gulf prawns), peeled (but tails left on) and de-veined

8 small metal skewers— or bamboo skewers, soaked in water for 30 minutes

200g bottled pesto

olive oil spray

ground black pepper

Put the prawns into a bowl with the pesto, coat well and marinate, refrigerate for 1 hour. Thread two prawns onto each skewer and place on a plastic wrap-lined plate. Spoon the pesto over, cover with plastic wrap and let sit for 4 hours in the refrigerator.

Spray a medium–hot flat plate with oil. Add the prawns and cook. Sprinkle on black pepper and baste once with the pesto. You can turn these twice during the cooking.

Serve on a platter with cocktail napkins to have as a starter around the barbecue.

PROSCIUTTO PRAWNS WITH ROCKET AIOLI

SERVES 4

16 large green king prawns, body shell removed and de-veined (heads and tails left on)

16 metal skewers—or bamboo skewers soaked in water for 30 minutes

8–16 slices prosciutto

rocket aioli (see page 48)

Take each prawn and thread it onto a skewer starting from the tail. Roll each prawn in prosciutto to cover all the prawn. Store on plastic wrap-covered plate in the refrigerator until ready to use. The size of the slice of prosciutto will depend on the size of the prawns being used.

Cook the prawns on a medium–hot flat plate turning regularly for even cooking. When the top (head end) of the prawns is completely white, they are ready to eat. The prosciutto wraps around the prawn very tightly as it cooks. Serve with a bowl of rocket aioli.

Garlic varies in its intensity and you need to be aware of this. In testing this recipe twice, with garlic from two different sources, I got two very different results. Go for large garlic cloves if they are not so powerful.

How do you find out about the intensity? Cut a small piece off the end of the garlic you are using and eat. If it is strong, cut back on the amount used—or blanch the garlic in boiling water for 30 seconds.

ROCKET AIOLI

4 medium garlic cloves

½ teaspoon sea salt

2 egg yolks

½ cup rocket, blanched
and well drained

125ml olive oil

1 teaspoon lemon juice

Put the garlic, salt, egg yolks and rocket into a food processor bowl and process for 30 seconds.

When this mixture is starting to thicken, slowly pour the oil down the feeder shoot. As it takes, you can add the oil a little more quickly until finished.

Use immediately or store for up to 5 days in the refrigerator. Stir in the lemon juice as you serve.

PRAWNS, ASPARAGUS AND MINT HOLLANDAISE

SERVES 4

16 green king prawns, peeled (but tails left on)

16 white or green asparagus spears, trimmed

vegetable oil spray

4 mint sprigs

mint hollandaise (see page 50)

Butterfly the prawns by nearly cutting through then slightly flatten. Spray the asparagus and prawns with oil and cook on medium–hot flat plate—turn the asparagus regularly for 3–4 minutes and grill until done.

Remove the asparagus and prawns from the barbecue and serve with the spears placed together in the centre of individual plates topped with 4 prawns. Spoon over a little sauce and decorate with a sprig of mint.

MINT HOLLANDAISE

1 tablespoon eschalot, finely chopped

1 teaspoon mint, dried

2 tablespoons fresh mint, chopped

2 tablespoons white vinegar

2 tablespoons white wine

2 egg yolks

120g firm butter, cut into cubes

1 teaspoon lemon juice

salt and cayenne pepper to taste

2 extra tablespoons mint, finely shredded

Make the sauce by putting the eschalots, dried mint, fresh mint, vinegar and white wine into a saucepan and boiling down by two thirds. Remove from the heat and tip into the top of a double boiler. Cool and add the egg yolks and whisk.

Put over the top of simmering water and whisk until the mixture thickens—as it does, start to whisk in the butter until all used. Remove from heat and pour in the lemon juice with salt and pepper to taste. Strain and stir in the extra mint.

SKEWERED PRAWNS, BARBECUED LEMON

SERVES 4

16 medium green king prawns, peeled and de-veined

bamboo skewers, soaked in water for 30 minutes or metal ones

4 lemon cheeks

olive oil

salt and pepper to taste

Insert the skewer into tail of the prawn and thread the meat on so that the flesh is kept straight. Arrange on a flat plate and drizzle over light olive oil. Rotate the prawns to coat them with oil.

Put the lemon cheeks onto the medium-hot grill, cut-side down, and cook for 1 minute.

Place the prawns on a medium-hot plate and cook for 3 minutes. Turn the prawns constantly and drizzle with the oil they have been sitting in. Sprinkle with salt and pepper.

To serve, remove the skewers from the prawns and put onto individual plates with a little side salad. Decorate with lemon cheek showing the barbecue marking. Alternatively, you can leave the skewers in and put on a platter, decorated with the lemon cheeks, and serve around the barbie as guests are assembling.

KING PRAWNS, MINT AND CHERVIL SAUCE

16 medium king prawns, completely peeled and deveined

2 tablespoons oil

½ teaspoon each of salt

½ lemon cracked pepper

mint and chervil sauce (see page 56)

Toss the prawns in oil, salt and lemon pepper. Sit for 15 minutes. Cook the prawns on a hot plate and turn regularly to cook through—they will take only a couple of minutes. Remove from the heat.

Serve the prawns on individual plates and with the sauce spooned over. Sprinkle with a little more cracked pepper to decorate.

MINT AND CHERVIL SAUCE

1 tablespoon eschalots, finely chopped

2 tablespoons fresh mint, chopped

1 tablespoon fresh chervil, chopped

1 small sprig fresh thyme

2 tablespoons white vinegar

2 tablespoons white wine

2 egg yolks

120g (4oz) firm butter, cut into cubes

½ teaspoon lemon juice

salt and cayenne to taste

1 tablespoon fresh mint, finely sliced

1 tablespoon chervil, finely chopped

Make the sauce by putting the eschalots, mint, chervil, thyme, vinegar and white wine into a saucepan and boil down by two thirds. Remove from the heat and tip into the top of a double boiler. Cool and add the egg yolks and whisk.

Put over the top of simmering water and whisk until the mixture thickens. As it does, start to whisk in the butter until all is used. Remove from heat and pour in the lemon with salt and cayenne to taste. Strain and stir in the mint and chervil.

ABALONE STRIPS WITH VIETNAMESE DIPPING SAUCE

SERVES 4

200g green lip abalone or cocktail abalones

ground black pepper

2 tablespoons peanut oil

sea salt

DIPPING SAUCE

1 teaspoon white sugar

2 tablespoons lime juice

1 tablespoon fish sauce

2 small red chillies, deseeded and minced

1 large clove garlic, minced

1 tablespoon rice vinegar

2–3 tablespoons water

Slice the abalone into fine slices about 3mm thick and tip into a bowl with ground black pepper to taste and oil—toss to coat and marinate for 15 minutes. Sometimes, depending on the abalone and its shape, it is best to put it into a freezer for about 15–20 minutes to get the flesh really set, but not frozen. Use a very sharp, thin knife to do the slicing.

Whisk the sauce ingredients together and pour into a serving bowl.

To barbecue, put the abalone strips onto a hot flat plate and cook in batches to avoid overcooking. The strips really only need to be on the hot plate for about 15 seconds each side or until the flesh is firm but not rock hard.

Remove from barbecue and serve around the bowl of sauce with toothpicks for lifting and dipping.

SKEWERED TUNA AND WASABI CREAM

SERVES 4

400g fresh tuna (not southern blue fin tuna)

12–16 metal skewers or bamboo skewers soaked in water for 30 minutes

60g plain yoghurt

2–3 tablespoons wasabi paste

1 tablespoon rice vinegar

1 tablespoon finely shredded mint

vegetable oil spray

sea salt

Cut the tuna into even pieces—you will get 12 to 16 pieces. Thread one piece only onto each skewer (don't leave the tip exposed) and refrigerate until ready to cook.

Mix the yoghurt, wasabi paste, vinegar and mint well—pour into dipping bowl.

Spray the tuna with oil and cook on medium–hot flat plate. Sprinkle with a little salt and spray with oil before turning to cook the other side.

Tuna loves to be undercooked. When you see the flesh— on the side of each piece—completely change colour to white, remove from heat for rare to medium tuna.

ASIAN-FLAVOURED SCALLOPS

SERVES 4

20 scallops, on shell

4 tablespoons green spring onions, minced

1 tablespoon kecap manis

1 teaspoon green ginger, finely minced

1 teaspoon lemongrass (white part only), minced

1 tablespoon lime juice

1 small green chilli, deseeded and minced

1/2 tablespoon water

Check each scallop to see that it is clean and grit free. Leave on shell and place on a large plate to take to barbecue.

Mix the remaining ingredients together and spoon a little over each scallop on the shell.

Place on a medium–hot, open grill. Cook a few at a time—they cook quickly. Lift from grill and spoon over a little more of the sauce. Serve when they are all cooked, which depends on their thickness.

SCALLOPS WITH PARSLEY AND MACADAMIA PESTO

SERVES 4

16 scallops

olive oil spray

sea salt

2 cups iceberg lettuce, finely shredded middle leaves only

1 cup ripe roma tomatoes, flesh only and finely diced

1 tablespoon dill, finely chopped

4 tablespoons parsley and macadamia pesto (see page 64)

ground black pepper

Trim the black membrane from the side of each scallop. Spray each one and cook on hot flat plate for 30 seconds to 1 minute each side, depending on the thickness of each scallop. Sprinkle with salt only as you cook.

To serve, put equal amounts of the finely shredded lettuce in small piles around the perimeter of individual dinner plates. Place scallops on top and sprinkle with tomato and dill.

Spoon the pesto into the centre of each plate, grind black pepper over the plate and serve immediately.

Scallops must not be overcooked as they go tough. They prefer to be seared rather than cooked through.

PARSLEY AND MACADAMIA PESTO

1 cup parsley sprigs, washed and tightly packed into the cup

1 tablespoon roasted, unsalted macadamia nuts, roughly chopped

$1/3$ cup macadamia nut oil

1 large cheese, finely grated

Put all ingredients into a processor and pulse until the ingredients start to break down. Process until a smooth paste is formed. Adjust the consistency of the pesto with more oil if needed.

THE BEST GARLIC BREAD

250g salted butter, room temperature

6 cloves garlic

3 tablespoons parsley, chopped

1 tablespoon lemon zest, finely grated

1 tablespoon lemon juice

½ tablespoon black pepper, freshly ground

1 loaf day-old bread of any type

Put all ingredients, except for the bread, into a large bowl or a processor. Combine well—if using a bowl, best to mash with a large fork and for the processor, just pulse until smooth. Lift out with a spatula and store or use.

The secret to the best garlic bread is to smear both sides of the bread and cook on a hot flat plate until lightly browned—finish by crisping on the open grill.

OCEAN TROUT BROCHETTES WITH SATAY DIPPING SAUCE

SERVES 4

16 x 30g pieces ocean trout, skinless and bones removed

16 small bamboo or stainless steel skewers (the larger, longer toothpicks are good)

vegetable oil spray

1/2 cup thick satay sauce

1/4 cup coconut cream

coriander leaves for decoration

Thread one piece of the fish onto the tip of each skewer—refrigerate until ready to cook.

Heat the satay sauce and coconut cream until warmed and combined then pour into dipping bowl.

Spray the ocean trout with a little oil (remembering that this fish has naturally good oil in it) and cook on a medium–hot flat plate for 30 seconds each side. Serve on a plate with the dipping sauce in the middle and decorated with coriander leaves.

ATLANTIC SALMON RISOTTO CAKES

SERVES 4

*500g basic risotto, cooled
(see page 166)*

*1 tablespoon lemon zest,
finely grated*

*100g Atlantic salmon,
boneless, skinless and
finely chopped*

2 eggs

½ cup plain flour

1 teaspoon dill, ground

breadcrumbs

olive oil spray

Mix the room temperature or chilled risotto with the zest, salmon, eggs, flour and dill—stir well. Divide the risotto into 24 equal portions and roll into balls. Flatten into rounds of 4cm in diameter and 2cm thick, then coat in breadcrumbs. Make sure all excess breadcrumbs are removed. Refrigerate until ready to use.

Spray the flat plate liberally with oil, add the cakes and cook for 1 minute. Spray liberally with oil, turn and cook for another minute on the other flat side. Serve as a 'pass around' or place in the middle of the table. A tossed salad served with them makes more of an appetiser.

The basic risotto with the salmon added is quite sticky, so it is best to divide the mixture into the 24 portions using a small ice cream scoop or a spoon dipped in water.
Dip your hands in water too before you roll and flatten the balls. I sometimes don't use the breadcrumbs and the cakes still cook.

MUSSELS AND TANDOORI DRESSING

SERVES 4

32 Kinkawooka black mussels (these are already scrubbed and debearded)

2 tablespoons tandoori paste

3 tablespoons natural yoghurt

2 tablespoons mint, finely chopped

mint leaves for decoration

Put the mussels onto a medium–hot open grill and soon they will start to open. Remove from grill, place into a large bowl and cool. Remove the top shells from the mussels and set to one side, reserving any juices that come from the mussels.

Mix the paste, yoghurt, mint and any reserved mussel juice. Place a half teaspoon onto each mussel—you may need more for larger mussels, but remember, in the cooking it will melt and ooze a little.

Put the mussels back on the medium–hot open grill and cook until they bubble around the sides. Serve immediately.

We eat these around the barbecue without the mint, but if you want to plate them to serve as a sit-down starter, you can decorate with mint leaves.

BOSTON BAY CLAMS IN BASIL AND WHITE WINE

SERVES 4

48 Boston Bay clams

2 spring onions, roughly chopped

2 cloves garlic, roughly chopped

2 bay leaves

12 peppercorns

1 cup dry white wine

2 cup fish stock

2 tablespoons Italian basil, chopped

3 tablespoons salted butter, very cold, diced into 3cm cubes

4–8 slices garlic bread

Make sure the clams are cleaned and ready for cooking. Put the onions, garlic, bay leaves and peppercorns into a stainless steel frying pan or similar. I have one that goes into the oven and the barbecue. If you have a domed lid for it, all the better.

Add the clams, wine and fish stock. If you have a lid, fit it on now and put onto a very hot open grill—if no lid, drop the hood and cook. If no hood or lid, cover with stainless steel bowl or similar. Bring to the boil and then simmer for 5 minutes.

Remove from the barbecue and distribute the clams into large individual bowls. Return pan to heat. Add the basil and cook for 30 seconds. Remove from the heat and swirl in the butter. Pour equal amounts over the clams and serve with garlic bread.

These clams grow in the pristine waters of Boston Bay in South Australia—they are all ready to go when you buy them.

Clams have been little used in Australia, but they are so good to eat and are becoming more popular.

SCALLOP AND BACON KEBABS

SERVES 4

16 scallops, roe removed

16 parsley, leaves only

16 x 10cm-long pieces bacon, rind removed

16 stainless steel skewers or bamboo skewers, soaked in water for 30 minutes

4 lemon cheeks

Remove the little black membrane from the side of each scallop.

Sit each scallop on the end of a piece of bacon—top with a parsley leaf and roll the bacon around each scallop. Thread 4 wrapped scallops onto each skewer.

Cook on medium–hot flat plate for 2 minutes each side and serve with the lemon cheeks.

As scallops are so delicate it is always good to offer them the protection of a wrap such as bacon.
Oh! and there's the flavour combo … yum!

SCALLOPS WITH BLOOD SAUSAGE AND PRAWN AND LIME BUTTER

SERVES 16

16 large scallops

16 x 2cm thick slices blood sausage

vegetable oil spray

2 cups creamy mashed potatoes, hot

fresh dill sprigs

4 x 1cm-thick slices prawn and lime butter (see page 77)

Trim the black membrane from the side of each scallop.

Cook the sausage slices very quickly on hot flat plate—remove and keep warm.

Spray scallops on both sides and cook very quickly on hot flat plate on both sides. Scallops like to be seared on both sides then lifted from the barbecue—to overcook them is to make them tough.

Spoon 16 dollops of potato mash around 4 individual plates. Top with a slice of sausage and then a scallop on top of the sausage. Decorate the plates with springs of dill in the middle and then top each scallop with a quarter slice of the prawn and lime butter. Serve immediately.

Scallops like to be seared on both sides then lifted from the barbecue—to overcook them is to make them tough.

PRAWN AND LIME BUTTER

250g salted butter, room temperature

60g cooked prawn meat, finely minced

1 tablespoon dill, finely chopped

1 tablespoon lime juice

1 teaspoon lime zest, finely grated

Mash all ingredients together in a bowl and when well combined, spoon onto a piece of plastic wrap and shape into a log/sausage. Roll, chill and freeze to keep. Slice down when ready to serve.

SCALLOPS AND ANCHOVY SAUCE

SERVES 4

16 scallops, roe on

¼ cup good mayonnaise

1 tablespoon lemon juice

1 tablespoon cold water

4 anchovy fillets, mashed

16 small sprigs dill

Trim the scallops by removing the black membrane from the side of the scallop.

Make the anchovy sauce by blending the mayonnaise, lemon juice, water, anchovies and dill to a smooth consistency.

Spray the scallops with oil and cook on a very hot plate for 1–1½ minutes. Turn and cook for no more than 1 minute on this side.

Spoon a small amount of the sauce into the base of Chinese spoons or dessert spoons. Place a scallop on top and spoon over a little of the sauce. Decorate with the dill sprig.

Serve on a platter with the handles facing to the rim.

CALAMARI WITH GREEN LENTIL AND MINT SALAD

SERVES 4

8 small calamari tubes

2 tablespoons olive oil

1 tablespoon parsley, chopped

sea salt

green lentil and mint salad (see page 81)

Cut the tubes open to form 8 large pieces. Score the flesh side with a very sharp knife to form diamond shapes—do not cut through the calamari; let the weight of the knife be enough pressure. The finer the diamonds, the quicker the calamari cooks. Cut the calamari into bite-sized pieces and tip into a bowl then add the oil and parsley and toss to coat. Let it marinate for 10 minute before cooking.

Cook quickly on a hot flat plate, moving the calamari around to expose all the flesh to the heat. Sprinkle with sea salt. Calamari cooks very quickly so do not let it overcook. Remove from barbecue and keep warm.

Scoop lentil salad into the centre of individual, flattish bowls, top with calamari and serve with good bread.

GREEN LENTIL AND MINT SALAD

2 cup cooked green lentils, drained and washed (I use canned green lentils)

1 small Spanish onion, roughly chopped

½ cup red capsicum, diced

1 cup mint leaves

½ cup mayonnaise

2 tablespoons sherry vinegar

1 teaspoon salt

½ teaspoon turmeric, ground

Combine the lentils, onion and capsicum. Tear the mint leaves into pieces and add them to the lentils. Whisk the mayonnaise, vinegar, salt and turmeric—pour over the lentils and stir well to combine flavours.

TUNA SLICES ON CUCUMBER WITH WASABI FLYING FISH ROE

SERVES 4

300g piece of tuna, completely trimmed

vegetable oil spray

sea salt

16 x 1cm-thick slices telegraph cucumber, on absorbent paper

2 tablespoons wasabi-flavoured flying fish roe

Cut the tuna into a log, about 3cm square. You may not be able to do this, but the idea is to be able to cut slices about 1cm thick to sit on the sliced cucumber.

Spray the tuna well with oil and sear on hot flat plate—turn regularly so you get even cooking on each side of the log. Cook for no more than 30 seconds on each side. Remove from heat and put on absorbent paper. Cool and refrigerate.

With a very sharp, thin knife, slice the seared tuna into 1cm-thick slices. Top each slice of cucumber with the tuna slice and top with the fish roe. Serve on cocktail napkins.

When buying tuna, ensure you don't buy southern blue fin tuna, which is being overfished.

There is no sustainable fishing of southern blue fin or yellowfin tuna.

CUTTLEFISH WITH SALSA VERDE AND BABY ROCKET

SERVES 4

300g cuttlefish tubes

¼ cup olive oil

2 tablespoons dill, chopped

salsa verde (see page 85)

100g baby rocket leaves

100g ripe tomatoes, diced

Cut each cuttlefish open to form a large piece and score into diamond shapes with a very sharp knife. Cut into bite-sized pieces and tip into a bowl with the olive oil and dill. Toss to coat and let sit for 10 minutes.

Drain the cuttlefish and cook on a hot flat plate until done. Move it constantly so that all flesh is exposed to heat—when done place into the salsa verde bowl and coat the cuttlefish. Let cool. To serve, put equal amounts of rocket and tomato onto individual plates and top with the salsa verde-coated cuttlefish.

Cuttlefish burns very easily. Move it constantly on the hot plate so all the flesh is exposed to the heat.

SALSA VERDE

2 cloves garlic, roughly chopped

2 cups parsley, tightly packed

1 tablespoon fresh oregano

1 tablespoon capers, rinsed

2 tablespoons white wine vinegar

1 tablespoon Dijon mustard

2 anchovy fillets

1/2 cup extra virgin olive oil

Put all ingredients except for the oil into a food processor and process—after 15 seconds or so start pouring in the oil.

You will have to stop once or twice to scrape the mixture down the side with a spatula. Work to a good paste. You may need extra olive oil or vinegar. Check the seasoning and spoon into a stainless steel or glass bowl.

THAI-INSPIRED FISH PATTIES

MAKES 12–15

500g white fish (e.g. snapper)

2 tablespoons garlic chives, washed and finely chopped

1 clove garlic, finely minced

1 tablespoon lemongrass (white part only), finely chopped

2 egg whites, lightly beaten

4 candle nuts or blanched almonds, roughly chopped

1/4 teaspoon nutmeg, grated

1/2 teaspoon dried shrimp paste

1 kaffir lime leaf, shredded

10 large coriander leaves, roughly chopped

1 tablespoon fish sauce

1 tablespoon rice flour

vegetable oil spray

4–8 lime cheeks

Finely mince the fish by pulsing in the food processor or putting through a mincing machine. Combine all ingredients except the oil and lime and mix well using your hands. Cover and refrigerate overnight.

After dipping your hands in cold water and leaving wet, shape the fish patties into the size you desire. I like mine around 6cm in diameter and around 2cm thick. Place onto a plastic wrap-lined plate, cover and refrigerate for 1 hour.

Spray the fish cakes liberally with oil and place them on a medium–hot flat plate, oiled side down, cook for 2 minutes.

Spray the patties with oil and turn to cook for a further 2 minutes. Lift from plate and serve on a platter with the lime cheeks as decoration and for squeezing.

You can serve these with some light soy sauce flavoured with a little sweet chilli dipping sauce or just with freshly squeezed lime juice.

SAL

ADS

WHILE WE MAY BE HAPPY JUST TO LIVE ON BARBECUED PRAWNS, FISH, LOBSTERS ... WHATEVER, NUTRITIONALLY WE MUST BALANCE OUT THE MEAL AND THAT'S WHERE SALADS COME INTO THE BARBECUE SCENE.

GONE ARE THE DAYS OF THE LETTUCE, BEETROOT AND ORANGE TWISTS.

TODAY WE WANT AND NEED SALADS WITH A LITTLE MORE GUSTO ... INDEED SALADS THAT WILL STAND UP AS A MEAL ON THEIR OWN.

THERE ARE SO MANY POSSIBILITIES FOR SALADS WITH THE RANGE OF VEGETABLES AND DRESSINGS TODAY. WHETHER YOU MAKE THE DRESSINGS YOURSELF OR SUPERMARKET SELECT, THE VARIATIONS ARE ENORMOUS.

KING PRAWN CAESAR SALAD

Serves 4

DRESSING

3 anchovy fillets, well drained of oil

2 egg yolks

2 large cloves garlic, minced

1 teaspoon Worcestershire sauce

1 tablespoon white vinegar

120ml olive oil

SALAD

24 medium sized green king prawns, peeled with tails on, de-veined and butterflied

oil spray

120g cos lettuce, inner whiter leaves, washed, crisped and cut into bite-sized pieces

2 hard boiled eggs, shelled and roughly chopped

4 tablespoons crisp bacon bits

50g shaved parmesan cheese

4 slices day-old sourdough

1 tablespoon garlic, crushed and mixed with 2 tablespoons olive oil

Make the dressing in the bowl in which you will serve the salad. Mash the anchovies with the back of a fork and add the egg yolks, garlic, Worcestershire and vinegar. Combine until lighter in colour and thickened. Whisk in the oil slowly to make a thick dressing.

Spray the prawns with oil and cook on medium–hot flat plate. Toss to cook through then remove and cool. Add the lettuce, eggs, bacon and cooled prawns to the dressing and toss to coat, then sprinkle on the cheese and croutons.

To make the croutons, cut the bread into 2cm squares. Heat the garlic oil to medium–hot in an ovenproof pan. Toss in the bread cubes and coat with the oil mixture. Put into a moderate oven until browned. Tip onto absorbent paper when done. They keep very well in an airtight container.

Serve salad in the middle of table.

CHARGRILLED HALOUMI, CARROT AND CHIVE SALAD

SERVES 4

300g carrots, peeled, halved lengthwise

½ cup orange juice

¼ cup walnut oil

½ teaspoon cumin, ground

½ teaspoon smoked paprika

¼ teaspoon chilli, ground

sea salt to taste

½ cup garlic chives, cut into 4cm-long pieces

haloumi, cut in 4 x 2cm-thick slices

olive oil spray

Cut the halved carrots into half moon shapes on the diagonal and boil for 2 minutes—drain and keep warm.

Whisk the orange juice with oil, cumin, paprika, chilli and salt. Add the carrots and chives and toss to combine. Tip into salad bowl.

Spray the haloumi with a little oil, cook on a medium–hot flat plate until lightly browned on each side. Spread around the top of the carrots and serve warm.

CHARGRILLED VEGETABLES AND PASTA SALAD WITH TOMATO BASIL DRESSING

SERVES 4

2 small carrots, peeled and cut in half lengthwise

2 small zucchini, trimmed and cut in half lengthwise

vegetable oil spray

3 x 2cm-thick onion slices, with toothpick through centre to hold in place

1 cup cauliflower, in florettes and blanched

8 teardrop tomatoes, halved

4 cups cooked spirali pasta, lightly oiled to stop it sticking together

1 cup tomato flesh, peeled and seeds removed

¼ cup olive oil

10 basil leaves, ripped

1 teaspoon green peppercorns, rinsed well

sea salt to taste

Spray the carrots and zucchini with vegetable oil and cook on a medium–hot flat plate until just cooked. Insert a skewer into them to test and, when soft but firm, remove and cool. Spray onion with oil and cook on medium heat on an open grill for 1 minute each side—remove and cool.

Put the cauliflower, teardrop tomatoes and pasta into a salad bowl. Cut the carrot and zucchini into bite-sized pieces and add to the pasta mix. Separate each onion ring and put in with the pasta.

Make the tomato dressing by blending the tomato flesh, oil, basil, peppercorns and salt in a blender or processor. When pureed, pour over the pasta and toss well to combine flavours. This is best done at least 4–5 hours beforehand and tossed hourly to combine flavours.

BARBECUED ASPARAGUS, EGG, OLIVE AND RED CAPSICUM DRESSING

SERVES 4

DRESSING

2 medium-sized red
capsicums

olive oil spray

2 tablespoons red wine
vinegar

2 tablespoons extra virgin
olive oil

sea salt and ground black
pepper to taste

SALAD

20 green asparagus spears

vegetable oil spray

2 eggs, hard-boiled

12 large green olives,
stuffed with almonds

1 cup Italian parsley,
loosely packed

1/2 cup Romano cheese,
shaved

Make the dressing first by cutting the cheeks of the capsicum away from the seed core. Spray the skin side with oil and cook on high on an open grill to blister the skin. Turn only once and cook for 1 minute on flesh side. Pop the cheeks into a plastic bag and let sit for 20 minutes so the skin lifts. Remove cheeks and peel away the skin.

Chop the skinned capsicum and put into a blender or food processor with the other dressing ingredients and blend to a puree.

Trim the asparagus of the white part and spray with oil. Cook on medium heat on an open grill—turn regularly for 2–3 minutes. Remove and cool.

Peel the eggs and cut into quarters. When the asparagus is cool enough to handle, cut into bite-sized pieces on an angle. Put into a salad bowl with the eggs, olives and parsley. Spoon over capsicum dressing to your taste, scatter the cheese over the top and serve.

CUMIN-INFUSED PUMPKIN, ZUCCHINI AND SPANISH ONION SALAD

SERVES 4

¼ cup olive oil

1 tablespoon cumin, ground

½ tablespoon rosemary, ground

½ teaspoon white pepper, ground

400g butternut pumpkin, peeled and cut into 2cm dices

200g zucchini, trimmed and cut into 2cm dices

1 medium Spanish onion, skin and roots on, cut into 8 wedges

8 toothpicks

olive oil spray

2 tablespoons extra virgin olive oil

1 tablespoon balsamic vinegar

½ cup baby watercress sprigs

Mix the oil, cumin, rosemary and pepper in a large bowl. Add the pumpkin and zucchini and toss to coat the pieces. Marinate for 20 minutes.

Spoon the pumpkin mix onto a medium–hot flat plate and turn and cook for around 5–10 minutes or until soft and browned. Spray the onion wedges and cook on the same plate for 5 minutes—they need to be cooked but still holding their structure. Remove from the heat and cool. Peel the skin away, remove the toothpicks and cut the roots off.

Drain the pumpkin mix on absorbent paper and tip into a large bowl. Add the onions, rosemary, oil and balsamic vinegar. Tumble to coat and mix flavours and let cool before serving. Decorate with the watercress and serve.

Put a toothpick lengthwise through the onion wedges to hold them in place when cooking—leaving the root on also helps.

RICE NOODLES AND BOK CHOY SALAD WITH GINGER CHILLI SOY DRESSING

Serves 4

SALAD

8 baby bok choy, halved, washed and well drained

vegetable oil spray

250g rice vermicelli noodles, rehydrated

60g green spring onions, roughly chopped

120g carrots, peeled and shredded

120g yellow banana capsicum, deseeded and cut into fine strips

2 tablespoons sesame seeds, toasted

DRESSING

2 tablespoons green ginger root, minced

2 tablespoons red chilli, minced and with seeds left in

1 clove garlic, minced

1 cup soy sauce

1 tablespoon honey

½ teaspoon sesame oil

To make dressing, whisk all ingredients together.

Wash the bok choy thoroughly and drain well. Spray cut side with oil and quickly cook (mark) on very hot open grill. I do this by putting the stalk part onto the grill but allowing the leaves to hang over the edge so that the softer green leaves do not dry out and burnt.

Remove from the grill and place around a large round platter with the grilled part in the centre of the plate.

Mix the noodles, spring onions, carrots and capsicum with half the dressing. Spoon onto the platter so that the noodles overlap some of the bok choy. Spoon the remaining dressing around and over the bok choy. Sprinkle with sesame seeds and serve immediately.

PUMPKIN, TOFU AND PINK GRAPEFRUIT SALAD

SERVES 4

300g Japanese pumpkin, skin on and cut into bite-sized pieces

olive oil spray

200g firm tofu, drained and cut into pieces around the same size as the pumpkin

2 pink grapefruit

½ cup olive oil

½ teaspoon honey

¼ teaspoon smoked paprika

sea salt and ground black pepper to taste

100g baby rocket leaves

Spray the pumpkin and tofu with oil and cook on a medium–hot flat plate—with the hood down or covered with large bowl—until done. Cool on absorbent paper.

Remove the skin from the grapefruit over a plate so you capture all juices. Cut the segments out of the membrane and set aside.

Whisk together the grapefruit juice, oil, honey, paprika, salt and pepper—it is good to have at least twice as much juice as oil and three times is even better. Put the pumpkin and tofu into the salad bowl, pour the grapefruit dressing over and gently toss with your hands. Let sit for 20 minutes.

When ready to serve, put the rocket in with the pumpkin and tofu. Toss to coat leaves. Clean down the inside of the bowl and spoon over the grapefruit segments and serve.

KUMARA WITH TUNA DRESSING

SERVES 4

SALAD

600g whole kumara

oil spray

100g Spanish onion,
finely chopped

1 cup celery, finely diced

1/2 cup mustard cress
leaves, loosely packed

DRESSING

180g canned tuna,
drained

1 1/2 cups mayonnaise

1 tablespoon white
vinegar

1/2 teaspoon sea salt

1/4 teaspoon white pepper

Prick the kumara all over with a dinner fork and cook in the microwave, on high, for 3 minutes. Remove and cool. Cut into 2cm-thick rounds, spray the flat surfaces with oil and cook on a medium–hot flat plate for 2 minutes each side. If you like, you can crisp them on the open grill, but be careful because they caramelise very quickly. Remove and cool on absorbent paper.

Make the dressing by blending or processing all ingredients to a smooth, creamy consistency.

Spread the kumara slices around a flat plate so they overlap. Spoon dressing over the top, sprinkle with the onion, celery and cress and serve.

FENNEL, BUTTER, GREEN BEAN AND ORANGE SALAD

Serves 4

150g butter beans, topped and tailed

150g green beans, topped and tailed

100g fennel bulb, raw and finely sliced

2 medium oranges, peeled and segmented (reserve juice)

¼ cup mint leaves, loosely packed

½ cup orange juice, incorporating reserved juices

2 tablespoons olive oil

sea salt and white pepper, ground, to taste

Blanch and refresh the beans—sit in large salad bowl. Add the fennel, orange segments and mint. Whisk the juice, oil, salt and pepper together and pour over the bean ingredients. Toss well and serve.

WATERCRESS, RADISH AND FETA SALAD WITH RASPBERRY AND TARRAGON DRESSING

Serves 4

4 cups watercress, washed, sprigs only and loosely packed

6 medium-sized red radish, trimmed

125g firm feta cheese

1 tablespoon lemon juice

2 tablespoons raspberry vinegar

2 tablespoons olive oil

3 tablespoons tarragon, finely chopped

1 teaspoon green peppercorns, rinsed and crushed

Tip the watercress into a salad bowl. Finely slice the trimmed radish and add to the bowl. Crumble or cut the cheese into the salad bowl.

Whisk the lemon juice, vinegar, oil, tarragon and peppercorns together well. Pour over the salad when ready to serve and toss well.

BARBECUED POTATO SALAD WITH ANCHOVY AND GARLIC DRESSING

SERVES 4

400g kipfler potatoes (Pink Fir Apple or baby Desiree will do too)

olive oil spray

3 green spring onions, white only and finely sliced

2 hard-boiled eggs, shells removed and roughly chopped

2 tablespoons crisp bacon pieces

3 tablespoons mint, roughly chopped

4 anchovy fillets, drained well

4 cloves garlic, poached for 5 minutes

1/2 cup good mayonnaise

1/4 cup white vinegar

1/2 teaspoon ground black pepper

Cut the potatoes on the diagonal into bite-sized pieces. Boil in salted water for 5 minutes—drain well and cool. When cool enough to handle, spray with oil and cook until tender on a medium–hot open grill.

Remove from the barbecue and tip into large mixing bowl. Add the spring onions, eggs, bacon and mint.

Mash the anchovies with the garlic. Stir in the mayonnaise, vinegar and ground black pepper to taste and pour over the potato mixture.

Toss to coat the ingredients and leave to cool. Refrigerate to use when needed.

This salad is made when the potatoes are warm and the day before use.

POTATO SALAD AND GARLIC DRESSING

SERVES 4

400g (14oz) Kifler potatoes (Pink Fir Apple or baby Desiree)

spray olive oil

3 green spring onions, white only and finely sliced

2 hard boiled eggs, shells removed and roughly chopped

2 tablespoons crisp bacon pieces

3 tablespoons mint, roughly chopped

4 cloves garlic, poached for 5 minutes

1/2 cup good mayonnaise

1/4 cup cider vinegar

1 teaspoon dried mustard

1/2 teaspoon ground black pepper

Cut the potatoes on the diagonal to give bite size pieces. Boil in salted water for 5 minutes. Drain well and let cool. When cool enough to handle, spray with oil and cook until tender on a medium–hot grill.

Remove from the barbecue and tip into a large mixing bowl. Add the spring onions, eggs, bacon and mint.

Mash the garlic and whisk in mayonnaise, vinegar, mustard and ground black pepper to taste and pour over the hot potato mixture.

Toss to coat the ingredients and leave to cool. Refrigerate to use when needed and this salad is best done when the potatoes are warm and made the day before use.

MA

ALL BARBECUE MEALS DEVELOP THEIR OWN PERSONALITY AND MEET DIFFERENT NEEDS. FOR EXAMPLE, YOU CAN ENTERTAIN WITH SOME 'SIT DOWN' ATTITUDE OR HAVE A FUN FAMILY BARBIE.

THE TRUE BEAUTY OF BARBECUES
IS THAT THEY ARE SO VERSATILE.

SOMETIMES YOU NEED DRESS-UP DISHES AND OTHER TIMES NOT—IT'S A SIT BACK AND RELAX TYPE OF MEAL. MODERN BARBECUES AND THEIR DIVERSE FUNCTIONAL DESIGNS MEAN WE CAN BE MORE ADVENTUROUS WITH OUR SEAFOOD BARBECUING.

INCREASINGLY, WOMEN ARE TAKING AN INTEREST IN BARBECUING—THE DAYS OF CREMATED CHICKEN AND CINDERED SAUSAGES ARE NUMBERED.

SEAFOOD ALLOWS WOMEN AND MEN TO SHOW OFF THEIR CREATIVITY. THAT CREATIVITY IS AIDED BY THE VAST RANGE OF SEAFOOD WE CAN BUY IN THIS MARVELLOUS COUNTRY OF OURS.

LOBSTER MEDALLIONS WITH THAI CUCUMBER AND ASIAN LEAVES

SERVES 4

8 medium-sized lobster medallions

¼ cup vegetable oil

¼ teaspoon sea salt

black pepper, ground, to taste

100g mixed Asian leaves

4 lemon cheeks

*Thai cucumber
(see page 118)*

Pat the lobster dry and brush both sides with oil. Cook on medium–hot open grill, sprinkle with salt and pepper. Turn when done—but only once as they cook through quite quickly—and season again. Remove from the barbecue and keep warm.

Distribute the leaves into the centre of individual dinner plates. Drain the cucumbers and toss over the leaves. Serve the lobster beside the salad—one piece flat and the other piece leaning against it. Decorate with lemon cheeks.

Turn lobster only once as they cook through quite quickly.

THAI CUCUMBER

SERVES 4

4 tablespoons coconut or rice vinegar

3 tablespoon white sugar

1 small red chilli, deseeded and minced

1 large Lebanese cucumber, seeds removed and finely diced

1 eschalot, finely diced

1 tablespoon green ginger root, minced

1 clove garlic, crushed

1 tablespoon coriander leaves, chopped

1 tablespoon vegetable oil

1 tablespoon fish sauce

Mix the vinegar and sugar together until sugar is dissolved. Add all the other ingredients, toss and marinate for 1 hour before serving.

SCALLOPS, CHICKEN AND VERMICELLI NOODLES

Serves 4

16 large scallops, roe on

300g chicken breast

plain flour for dusting

spray vegetable oil

300g rice vermicelli noodles, rehydrated

coriander leaves for decoration

DRESSING

200ml coconut cream

2 cloves garlic, minced

½ teaspoon ginger, minced

2 small red chillies, split through but not cut in half

3 kaffir lime leaves

5 sprigs coriander, finely broken or chopped

2 teaspoons fish sauce

½ teaspoon sesame oil

½ tablespoon palm sugar

1 small lemon, juiced

coriander leaves for decoration

Remove the black membrane from each scallop. Cut the chicken into 2cm-thick round slices. Refrigerate both until ready to cook. In a wok, over medium heat, add the coconut cream, garlic, ginger, red chillies, kaffir lime leaves (crush them as you put them in), coriander, fish sauce, sesame oil, sugar and lemon juice. Bring to the simmer and cook for 10 minutes. Put the flour into a plastic bag and toss the chicken slices in it. Lift the slices out and shake off all excess flour.

Have the coconut dressing simmering on the wok/cooking ring on the barbecue. Spray the flat plate with oil and sear the chicken. Place in coconut mixture. Spray the scallops lightly with oil and sear on a hot flat plate. Place in the coconut mixture. Simmer for 10 minutes—ensure the chicken is cooked through.

To serve, lift out the kaffir lime leaves and the chillies. Put equal amounts of the vermicelli noodles into bowls, spoon over the scallops and chicken and all the dressing and decorate with the coriander leaves.

LIME LOBSTER WITH CRUSTY POTATOES AND ASPARAGUS

SERVES 4

500g green lobster meat, in 3cm-thick slices or chunks

1 teaspoon lime zest, finely grated

1 lime, juiced

¼ teaspoon sea salt

8 baby Pontiac potatoes, skin on, par boiled for 5 minutes and cooled

2 tablespoons olive oil

black pepper, ground, to taste

20 large asparagus spears, trimmed

olive oil spray

1 teaspoon fresh black pepper, finely ground

60g butter, melted and lightly browned

Soak the lobster meat in the zest, lime juice and salt for no more than 10 minutes.

Squash or slightly flatten the potatoes using the palm of your hand or a potato masher.

Pour some olive oil onto a medium–hot flat plate and gently place the potatoes on the plate—I use a spatula to do this. Sprinkle with pepper and drizzle with a little more oil and bring down the lid or cover with a stainless steel bowl. After 5 minutes turn the potatoes over gently as they can break easily.

Spray the asparagus with oil and cook on the grill but lay them across the grill so the spears don't fall into the open slats and turn regularly so they don't burn. Remove when ready, along with the crisped potatoes. Keep both warm.

Drain the lobster pieces and pour a little more olive oil onto the flat plate. Add the lobster and drizzle on lime juices from the soaking and half the butter. Turn and toss the lobster constantly until cooked through.

Remove from barbecue and assemble dish by placing two potatoes into the centre of each plate, stand equal quantities of asparagus against them and spoon lobster pieces over the base of the asparagus. Spoon remaining butter over the lobster and serve immediately.

DILL AND PEPPER-CRUSTED BLUE EYE WITH GOAT CHEESE SALAD

SERVES 4

4 x 170g blue eye fillets

1 tablespoon dill seeds

½ tablespoon white peppercorns

¼ teaspoon sea salt

spray olive oil

GOAT CHEESE SALAD

150g mixed salad leaves

100g semi roasted tomatoes, chopped

100g dry goat cheese, crumbled or cut into dice

3 tablespoons extra virgin olive oil

1 tablespoon balsamic vinegar

Pat the fish fillets dry. Roughly crush the dill seeds, peppercorns and salt in a mortar and pestle. Sprinkle equal amounts onto each side of the fish and pat into each fillet.

Heat half the flat plate to high, spray each fillet with oil and put onto that part. Spray with oil and turn after a minute. Leave there for another minute and then move to a medium–hot part of the flat plate to let them cook through. Remove when done—the fish will be firm to touch but not breaking up.

Serve the fish on individual plates—with the goat cheese salad in the middle of the table—and lots of good crusty bread.

To make the salad, place the leaves, tomatoes and cheese in a bowl and toss with the oil and balsamic vinegar.

FLATHEAD TAILS WITH SOFT MUSHROOM POLENTA AND MINT LEMON PESTO

SERVES 4

4-8 flathead tails

olive oil spray

2 cups mint leaves, loosely packed

2 tablespoons lemon juice

1 clove garlic, roughly chopped

1 tablespoon pine nuts

1 tablespoon parmesan cheese, finely grated

125ml olive oil

3 cups chicken stock

1 cup yellow polenta

½ cup mushrooms, small and white as possible and finely chopped

sea salt to taste

30g butter

Trim the tails off the fin, refrigerate until ready to cook.

Put the mint leaves, juice, garlic, pine nuts and cheese into a food processor. Start the motor and slowly add the oil in a steady stream. Set aside.

Make the polenta by bringing the stock to the boil and then tipping the polenta in slowly as you stir with either a wooden spoon or a whisk. Tip in the mushrooms. Keep cooking over medium heat until the polenta is soft, around 5 minutes. Remove from heat and stir in the salt and butter. Keep warm.

Spray the fish and cook, with the hood down, on a medium–hot flat plate until done. They tell you when they are ready as they will exude a white liquid from around the bone when ready to go. Turn regularly as you cook.

Spoon the polenta into the middle of individual plates, lean the fish tail against the polenta. Spoon a tablespoon or two of the mint pesto beside the fish and serve.

SEARED TUNA AND GREEN MANGO SALAD

SERVES 4

4 x 150g tuna steaks

2 tablespoons black peppercorns, crushed

vegetable oil spray

2 medium green mangoes or green apples

1/2 teaspoon salt

1 tablespoon fish sauce

1 tablespoon palm sugar, grated

1 tablespoon vegetable oil

3 tablespoon pre-cooked eschalots (available in Asian supermarkets)

4 green spring onions, trimmed and sliced diagonally to bite-sized pieces

1/2 teaspoon ground white pepper

3 tablespoons roasted macadamia nuts, roughly crushed

1 large green chilli, deseeded and finely sliced

Lightly crust the tuna with the pepper and refrigerate until ready to cook.

Peel the mangoes and slice from the seed—slice very finely into half moon shapes. If using apples, remove from the core and slice very finely. Place the slices into a bowl, sprinkle with salt and toss together. Mix the fish sauce, palm sugar and oil together and pour over the mango or apple slices. Add the eschalots, green spring onions, pepper and macadamias—toss gently to combine.

Spray the tuna with oil and cook on medium–hot flat plate for a minute—spray with some more oil and turn and cook for 30 seconds. You can continue cooking on the flat plate or at this stage move to the open grill to get more flavour and to get the 'grill marks'.

Don't let the tuna overcook whatever you decide to do. It is best served medium and the cooking time depends on the thickness of the tuna steak.

Spoon the mango or apple salad into individual large Asian bowls, top with the tuna and sprinkle with the green chilli slices.

SOY-SOAKED CORAL TROUT STRIPS AND GLASS NOODLE SALAD

SERVES 4

400g coral trout fillets

½ cup soy sauce

2 tablespoons vegetable oil

1 clove garlic, crushed

1 tablespoon green ginger root, peeled and minced

1 teaspoon white sugar

2 tablespoons fresh pineapple juice

vegetable oil spray

glass noodle salad (see page 127)

Cut the fish into even-sized strips.

Mix all the remaining ingredients together (except for the oil spray and coriander leaves) and add the fish strips—coat well and marinate for 20 minutes.

Drain the fish and cook on oil sprayed medium–hot flat plate. Turn pieces gently as they are fragile.

Serve equal amounts over the top of individual bowls of the noodle salad.

I make my pineapple juice by pulverising the flesh with a hand processor in a large jar then straining the juice for the pulp. Glass noodles are also known as mung bean noodles— these noodles are made of mung bean and tapioca starch.

GLASS NOODLE SALAD

SERVES 4

125g dried bean thread
noodles

100g daikon (Japanese
white radish), peeled and
finely shredded

½ telegraph cucumber,
cut lengthwise and then
into half moons

1 very small Spanish
onion, peeled and sliced
very finely

50g Japanese pickled
ginger, finely sliced

1 cup snow pea sprouts,
washed and crisped

coriander leaves for
decoration (optional)

DRESSING

1 tablespoon palm sugar

100 ml coconut cream

2 limes, juiced

1–2 tablespoons fish
sauce (nam pla)

Put the noodles into a large bowl and pour boiling water over to cover them—let sit for 5–10 minutes and then strain. Run under cold water to stop cooking. Ensure all the water is removed and tip the noodles into a mixing bowl and allow to cool for 10 minutes.

Add all the other ingredients except for the coriander leaves and toss gently using your hands.

Make the dressing by combining all the ingredients and mixing well. Pour over the assembled salad ingredients and toss gently. Top with the coriander leaves and serve as a side salad as above.

MIXED SEAFOOD LINGUINE

4 small fillets fish (e.g. whiting)

8 medium king prawns, peeled, de-veined and butterflied

olive oil spray

12 mussels, out of shell

8 small sea scallops, cleaned and black membrane removed

12 Pacific oysters, out of shell

2 tablespoons olive oil

2 tablespoons butter

1 small onion, finely chopped

400g canned crushed tomatoes

1 cup white wine

2 cloves garlic, chopped

oregano or marjoram to taste

sea salt and pepper to taste

600g linguine, cooked al dente

ciabiatta, sliced

Make sure all the seafood is cleaned and ready to cook; store covered in the refrigerator. In the kitchen, make the sauce by heating the oil and butter in a saucepan (I use a wok). When foaming add the onion and stir for 2 minutes. Pour in the crushed tomatoes, wine and garlic, simmer for 30 minutes. Remove from heat and keep warm if using shortly; otherwise, cool, cover and refrigerate.

When ready to serve, add the oregano or marjoram, salt and pepper to the sauce and take it to the barbecue along with the linguine and raw seafood. Heat the sauce on the ring, stir, add the mussels and simmer. Cook the fish and prawns by spraying with a little oil and cooking on a medium–hot flat plate until done.

Meanwhile add the scallops and oysters to the sauce and stir in. Carefully add the linguine and reheat using tongs to lift and stir. Remove the cooked seafood from the barbecue and keep warm. Serve the pasta and sauce into large individual bowls. Place a cooked fillet on the pasta and top with the prawns. Put the bread into the middle of the table and serve with a good green salad.

MONKFISH WITH GREEN BEAN, BACON AND APPLE SALAD

SERVES 4

4 x 180g pieces monkfish

olive oil spray

200g green beans, topped and tailed, blanched and refreshed

1 small Spanish onion, finely diced

1 green apple, cored and finely shredded

150g bacon pieces, 3cm long, rind removed and crisped on the barbecue

½ cup macadamia nuts, roasted and unsalted, roughly chopped

½ cup macadamia mayonnaise (see page 131)

¼ cup chervil leaves

black pepper, ground

Trim the fish if necessary. Spray with oil and cook on medium–hot flat plate until done.

Toss the beans, onion, apple, bacon and nuts with the mayonnaise and lemon juice. Add the chervil leaves as you do the final toss, with ground black pepper to taste.

Pile equal amounts of bean salad into the centre of individual plates and top with fish. Serve with good sourdough bread.

If you ever wondered why green beans look so green in cookbook photographs it is because they are 'blanched and refreshed'. Plunge the trimmed green beans into boiling water and boil for 1 minute—longer if you have a lot to do. Remove from the water and plunge in iced water to cool. This stops the cooking process very quickly and maintains the green colour.

MACADAMIA MAYONNAISE

3 large egg yolks, room temperature

¼ teaspoon salt

white pepper, pinch

½ teaspoon prepared mustard (smooth Dijon is best)

1 teaspoon white vinegar

250ml macadamia oil

Place the egg yolks, salt, pepper, mustard and vinegar into a food processor—work for 30 seconds or until the mixture in light in colour.

Drip the oil in, drop by drop, until you have a third of the oil added and then slowly increase the flow of oil to a steady thin stream until all oil has been incorporated.

If you add the olive oil too quickly, the mayonnaise will curdle. Should this happen, tip in 1 teaspoon of hot water and continue to add a little more oil to the mixture.

Egg yolks cook very quickly so, if you are doing a warm egg yolk sauce and the yolks look as though they will curdle, drop an ice cube into the mixture and whisk away from the heat.

DUKKAH-CRUSTED ATLANTIC SALMON WITH TABBOULEH SALAD

SERVES 4

4 x 180g Atlantic salmon fillets, skinless and bones removed

olive oil spray

1 cup dukkah (see page 133)

4 lemon cheeks

TABBOULEH

1½ cups spiced bulgur mix (I use Samir's Bulgur Feast mix)

1 cup cold water

2 cup parsley, chopped

1 cup ripe tomatoes, diced

1 tablespoon lemon zest, finely shredded

3 tablespoons lemon juice

2 tablespoons extra virgin olive oil

Soak the bulgur mix in the water for 30 minutes. Add the other salad ingredients and mix thoroughly. I like to leave this mixture to sit for at least 3 hours before use. Why do I use the Samir mix? All the spices are in the mix and it saves you time and having to shop for all the ingredients.

Evenly slice the fillets (if you have bought them already in 180–200g pieces) into pieces around 2–3 cm thick. Spray flesh side lightly with oil and press into dukkah on flat dinner plate. Lift and shake off excess. Spray medium–hot flat plate with oil and cook the fillets dukkah-side down first.

After a minute, spray the other side of the fish pieces, and with a long spatula, gently flip the fish over. The cooking time will depend on the thickness of the pieces.

Put the salad onto individual plates and top with equal amounts of fish and serve with cheeks to one side.

DUKKAH

MAKES 1½ CUPS

100 almonds, skin on

60g pine nuts

20g linseeds

1 teaspoon coriander, ground

1 teaspoon cumin, ground

1 teaspoon white sesame seeds

½ teaspoon chilli powder

1 teaspoon Szechuan peppercorns

Dry roast the almonds then the pine nuts and linseeds over medium heat. Cool and tip in a food processor. Add the coriander, cumin, sesame seeds, chilli and Szechuan pepper and work to a rough mixture—it should be granular/lumpy and not a paste. Store in an airtight container.

Dry roasting is where the nuts and seeds are pan-fried dry without any added moisture or fat—this brings out flavours and natural oils.

MEXICAN SPICED OCEAN TROUT FAJITAS

SERVES 4

500g ocean trout fillets, skin and pin bones removed

2 tablespoons of corn oil (or light olive oil)

2 tablespoons white vinegar

1 teaspoon Mexican chilli powder

1 teaspoon allspice, ground

½ teaspoon oregano, ground

olive oil spray

8 wheat flour tortillas

2 cups shredded lettuce

1 small Spanish onion, finely sliced

1 cup carrot, grated

red Tabasco sauce (optional)

Cut the fish into 2cm wide x 8cm long strips; mix the oil, vinegar, chilli powder, allspice and oregano in a bowl and add the fish strips. Cover and refrigerate for 20 minutes.

Spray a medium–hot flat plate with oil, and add the strips. Spread them evenly and do only as many as you can control. As ocean trout does not like to be overcooked, I normally cook 10 strips at a time and turn them only once. Remove from heat and keep warm.

Spray the tortillas with oil and heat very quickly, 30 seconds each side, on the hot open grill. Remove and stack on plate.

Assemble fajitas by putting fish strips near the middle of each tortilla, top with lettuce, onion and grated carrot.

Roll and eat immediately. You can drizzle on some Tabasco sauce if you like.

JEWFISH (MULLOWAY) STEAKS WITH BLOOD ORANGE AND BEETROOT SALAD

SERVES 4

4 x 180g jewfish steaks

2 tablespoons fresh thyme, chopped

ground black pepper to taste

olive oil spray

Trim the fish if necessary and pat the thyme into each side with ground black pepper to taste. Spray the fish with oil and cook on a medium–hot flat plate—this fish cooks very quickly and goes mushy if overcooked. The steaks go white along the side and when halfway up the sides of each steak, turn to cook for another minute.

When the steak is firm to the press of your middle finger or tongs, remove from the barbecue. Heap salad into the middle of dinner plates and serve the fish on top.

BEETROOT, BLOOD ORANGE AND MUSTARD DRESSING

SERVES 4

500g beetroot, medium size, cooked and skin removed

4 blood oranges

2 tablespoons smooth French mustard

2 tablespoons dill leaves, chopped

½ tablespoon fennel seeds, toasted and roughly crushed

reserved orange juice

Cut the cooled beetroot into wedges. Slice the skin and pith (white part of orange skin) from 3 of the oranges and cut into wedges. Do this on a plate so you reserve the juices.

Juice the remaining whole blood orange and combine with the reserved juices—whisk in the mustard. Combine the beetroot and oranges—add the dill and fennel seeds. Spoon the dressing over and tumble gently before serving.

Beetroot is best covered in boiling water while cooking. Sit in water to cool for around 10 minutes then lift out and rub skin off with your hands in plastic gloves.

They can also be roasted in loosely-wrapped foil, which is rubbed against the skin to remove it after the beetroot are cooked and cool enough to handle.

Beetroot around the size of tennis balls take about 25 minutes to cook by boiling and around 45 minutes when roasting in foil.

PRAWNS WITH LAKSA SAUCE

SERVES 4

24 large green king prawns, completely peeled and de-veined (keep shells and heads for stock)

vegetable oil spray

SAUCE

3 x 10cm stalks lemongrass, white part only, roughly chopped

3cm galangal, peeled and roughly chopped

3cm green ginger root, peeled and roughly chopped

2 small red chillies, seeds in and roughly chopped

2 tablespoons vegetable oil

1 tablespoon curry powder

1 teaspoon (or to taste) chilli sauce

2 teaspoons tamarind puree

$1^{1}/_{2}$ cups coconut milk

$^{1}/_{2}$ tablespoon fish sauce

ground white pepper and white sugar to taste

2 tablespoons lightly browned desiccated coconut

3 cups cooked vermicelli noodles

GARNISH

2 sliced eschalots

1 sliced lime

1 small Lebanese cucumber, shredded

1 cup Vietnamese mint leaves

Make a stock using prawn heads and shells with 3 cups water; simmer to reduce to 1 cup. Put the lemongrass, galangal, ginger and chillies into a food processor and work into a paste (you may need to add a little oil)—or use a mortar and pestle.

Heat oil in a wok and fry lemongrass paste mixture for 2 minutes. Add 1 cup prawn stock, curry powder, chilli sauce and tamarind puree—bring to a simmer to cook for 2 minutes. Pour in the coconut milk—season to taste with fish sauce. Ground white pepper can be used if you like and sugar can be used to taste to balance out the flavours.

Barbecue the prawns by spraying with a little oil and cooking on a hot open grill. Remove from barbecue when done and keep warm. Add the desiccated coconut to the coconut sauce and mix to thicken it. Simmer for 2 minutes and serve over equal amounts of cooked noodles in individual bowls.

Top with an equal amount of prawns and serve immediately. Serve the garnish of sliced eschalots, sliced limes, shredded cucumber and Vietnamese mint on a separate plate. This can be added to the prawn dish or eaten on its own.

BABY SNAPPER WITH CHEESY CREAMY POTATOES AND MINTED PEAS

SERVES 4

4 plate-sized baby snappers

1 small lemon, cut into quarters

12 garlic chives

80g butter, melted

1 teaspoon sea salt

1 teaspoon cracked black pepper

4 large sheets of aluminium foil, sprayed with oil

200g peas, frozen or fresh

1 tablespoon butter

3 tablespoons mint, finely chopped

cheesy creamy potatoes (see page 142)

Wash the fish cavity with cold water and dry with absorbent paper. Cut 2 deep slashes into each side of each fish. Place the fish on individual pieces of oiled foil—stuff the cavity with the lemon quarter and 3 garlic chives, cut to fit the cavity.

Spoon over the melted butter and sprinkle with salt and pepper. Repeat for each fish. Wrap the fish in the foil and refrigerate for 30 minutes. Ensure that the foil is tight around the fish so the juices cannot escape in the cooking process.

Bring the fish to room temperature for 15 minutes before placing them on a medium–hot flat plate and cooking for 6–7 minutes each side.

Remove from plate and serve on individual dinner plates. Cover the peas with water and boil for 2–3 minutes, strain and return to saucepan with butter and mint. Put on lid and toss to coat the peas with butter and mint. Turn out into serving bowl. Put the cheesy creamy potatoes and peas into the middle of the table.

CHEESY CREAMY POTATOES

1kg potatoes, washed (use Pontiac or regular ones)

1 tablespoon butter

125g onion, finely chopped

100ml cream whisked with 350ml milk

sea salt to taste

ground white pepper to taste

125g Gruyere cheese, grated

Slice the potatoes very finely (use a knife or mandolin)—put into water to stop browning.

Grease a suitably sized ovenproof dish with the butter and sprinkle in a layer of onion then layer in half the potatoes. Pour in half the cream/milk mixture. Wriggle/shake the dish so the liquid goes all the way through and sprinkle with a little salt and pepper. Add the last of the onion and the potatoes and the cream and milk.

Sprinkle with a little more salt and pepper, top with the cheese and cook at 180°C for 1 hour or until soft when a sharp knife is inserted. Remove from oven to serve.

PEPPERED MONKFISH WITH ASPARAGUS AND BRAISED BORLOTTI BEANS

SERVES 4

4 x 180g pieces monkfish

black pepper, ground

olive oil spray

16 asparagus spears, trimmed

BRAISED BORLOTTI BEANS

300g borlotti beans, rehydrated

100g onion, finely chopped

3 cloves garlic, minced

400g canned crushed tomatoes

¼ cup tomato paste

1 small piece dried mandarin skin

sea salt and ground black pepper to taste

¼ cup parsley, finely chopped

Trim the fish if necessary, refrigerate until ready for use.

Grind black pepper liberally over both sides of the fish, spray with oil and cook on medium–hot flat plate. Cook until done, which depends on the thickness of the fish.

Spray the asparagus spears with oil and cook on open grill—turn regularly.

Cover the beans with water and simmer for 45 minutes.

Put the onion, garlic, tomatoes, tomato paste and mandarin skin into a large saucepan and bring to the boil. Simmer and add the drained beans and continue simmering for at least 30 minutes. Season with salt, pepper and parsley and cook a further 5 minutes.

Serve by spooning equal amounts of the braised beans into the centre of individual flattish bowls then top with equal quantities of asparagus and fish.

BREAM FILLETS WITH SNOW PEAS AND GARLIC POTATO BAKE

SERVES 4

4 x 180g bream fillets, best is silver, black or yellowfin

oil spray

sea salt

300g snow peas, trimmed

4 lemon cheeks

garlic potato bake (see page 146)

Trim the fish if necessary. Spray the skin side with oil and sprinkle on a little sea salt. Put fish, skin side down, onto a hot flat plate and press down with a spatula, which prevents the fillet from curling. Repeat with all the fillets, spray the flesh side with oil and turn after 1–2 minutes. The skin can go quite crispy and the cooking time will depend on the thickness of the fillets.

Drop the peas into boiling salted water and cook for 1–2 minutes depending on their size. Thinner ones take much less time to cook through. Strain and serve immediately.

Place a wedge of the potato bake with the point in the centre of each plate. Put a pile of peas around that point and place a piece of fish, skin side up, on the peas, with the lemon to one side.

Sea bream, sometimes called morwong, is on the overfished list of fish, so be aware of this when buying your bream.

GARLIC POTATO BAKE

30g butter

1 tablespoon olive oil

3 leeks, white only,
cleaned and sliced thinly

4 cloves garlic, chopped

300ml pouring cream

4 large potatoes, peeled
and sliced thinly

salt and pepper to taste

3 tablespoons chopped
parsley

Pan fry leeks in foaming butter and oil until soft. Add garlic, stir, add cream and reduce until thick. Place potatoes in a bowl and pour over creamed leek, season with salt and pepper, parsley and mix gently.

Line a heavy oven dish or ovenproof frying pan with baking paper and press in potatoes. Bake in a moderate oven for about 1 hour.

When cooked, allow to cool slightly before turning out and slicing into wedges. This can be made in advance.

BLUE EYE WITH PEA MASH AND CABERNET JUS

SERVES 4

4 x 180g blue eye pieces

ground black pepper

olive oil spray

250g pontiac potatoes, cooked and mashed

200g green peas, cooked

2 tablespoons mascarpone

120g extra green peas, cooked

100ml cabernet jus, heated

EASY CABERNET JUS

2 tablespoons onion, finely diced

½ cup cabernet sauvignon wine

1 teaspoon sage, ground

1 packet (165g) red wine and garlic prepared liquid gravy

25g unsalted butter

Trim the fish if necessary, spray with oil and cook on medium–hot flat plate—sprinkle with ground black pepper. Cook until done—depending on the thickness of the fish. Combine the hot mashed potatoes, peas and mascarpone and mash well.

Simmer onion in the red wine until volume reduced to half. Add the sage, pour in the gravy and simmer for 5 minutes. When ready to use, swirl in the butter.

Serve by spooning equal amounts of pea mash into the centre of individual flattish bowls, top with cooked fish and spoon jus around the base of the pea mash. Sprinkle the extra peas onto the jus and serve.

BUG TAILS WITH ASIAN SLAW

SERVES 4

400g green (raw) bug tails, meat only

2–4 pineapple slices, fresh, cored and cut into pieces

8 stalks lemongrass

1 tablespoon soy sauce

¼ teaspoon sesame oil

Asian slaw (see page 149)

4 lime wedges

De-vein the bug tails and cut into pieces similar in size to the pineapple pieces and alternatively thread, with the pineapple pieces, onto the lemongrass stalks and refrigerate.

Mix the soy sauce with the sesame oil. Brush the bug skewers with the soy mixture and place on the medium–hot flat plate and baste twice while cooking.

Spoon Asian slaw onto the centre of four individual plates and top with bug skewers and decorate with lime wedges.

ASIAN SLAW

300g Chinese cabbage (wom bok)

2 green spring onions

1 clove garlic

100g green capsicum

1 small red chilli, de-seeded

50g roasted peanuts, roughly crushed

2 limes, juiced

½ tablespoon rice oil

1 tablespoon fish sauce

Finely slice the cabbage, spring onions, garlic, capsicum and chilli, mix with the nuts. Whisk the lime juice, oil and fish sauce and pour over the cabbage, fold through.

OCEAN TROUT WITH POTATO MASH, CHARRED RADICCHIO AND BEURRE ROUGE

SERVES 4

4 x 180g pieces ocean trout

½ cup melted butter

300g Pontiac potatoes (or similar), peeled and chopped

60g mascarpone

sea salt and cayenne pepper to taste

2 small radicchio, washed thoroughly and halved from root to top

spray olive oil

beurre rouge (see page 154)

Trim the fish if necessary. Refrigerate until ready to use.

Boil the potatoes until really well cooked then drain, put lid back on and leave sit for 5 minutes. Mash with the mascarpone, salt and cayenne to taste.

Brush the fish with butter and put onto a medium–hot flat plate, flesh side down, for 1–2 minutes. Brush skin side with butter and turn to cook until done to your liking. I prefer medium and the cooking time depends on the thickness of your fish.

Spray the cut side of radicchios and cook them quickly on a very hot open grill, then remove.

Put the radicchios cut side down on outer part of individual dinner plates, spoon potato mash beside the radicchio base, place the fish standing against the potato and radicchio base. Spoon the sauce around the base of all the ingredients and serve immediately.

BARRAMUNDI FILLET WITH GREEN CURRY SAUCE AND QUICK STIR-FRIED RICE

SERVES 4

4 x 180g pieces barramundi fillet

vegetable oil spray

½ cup Thai green curry paste

1 cup coconut milk

300g snake beans, trimmed

quick stir-fried rice (see page 155)

Trim the fish if necessary and refrigerate until ready to cook.

Mix the curry paste and coconut milk in a saucepan and simmer for 5 minutes. Stir occasionally.

Cut the snake beans into bite-sized pieces and boil until tender. Drain and keep warm.

Spray both sides of the fish with oil and cook on a medium–hot flat plate. The time will depend on the thickness of each piece but barramundi cooks quickly, so do watch it carefully.

Spoon rice onto individual plates and pile snake beans alongside the rice. Place fish beside the rice opposite the beans and spoon over the green curry sauce to taste. Me, I love it and have lots, but it's up to you how much you serve.

BEURRE ROUGE

1 cup chicken or fish stock

½ cup red wine (shiraz preferably)

1 tablespoon onion, finely chopped

200g unsalted butter, very cold and in 3cm cubes

Make the sauce by simmering the stock, red wine and onion until the liquid has reduced by three-quarters. Remove from the heat and swirl in each cube of butter to combine to a thickish red wine sauce.

Serve as soon as possible.

Perhaps the idea of serving a red wine sauce with fish is new to you but this sauce is delicious and smooth. It needs to be made for the meal, but the base can be done beforehand and reheated before swirling in the butter.

QUICK STIR-FRIED RICE

1 tablespoon vegetable oil

3 rashers bacon, rind removed and diced

4 green spring onions, white part minced, green tops reserved

2 cloves garlic, minced

4 cups long grain rice, cooked

3 tablespoons soy sauce

Heat the oil in a wok and add the bacon. Stir fry for 2 minutes or until it starts to crisp.

Add the white part of the spring onions with the garlic. Stir and cook for another minute.

Tip in the rice and stir through to reheat. Pour in the soy and combine well.

Remove from the heat and chop some of the reserved green tops of the spring onion and stir through. Serve immediately.

SPANISH MACKEREL KEBABS WITH MANGO AND LYCHEE SALSA

SERVES 4

600g Spanish mackerel
fillets

1 tablespoon sesame seeds

½ tablespoon sesame oil

1 tablespoon rice oil

¼ cup soy sauce

1 cup mango flesh, diced

½ cup lychees, deseeded
and diced

¼ cup green spring
onions, finely diced

¼ cup lime juice

8 coriander leaves,
roughly chopped

1 teaspoon fish sauce

1 large green fruity chilli,
minced

coriander leaves for
decoration

Cut the mackerel into even sized pieces. Thread equal quantities onto oiled stainless skewers. Refrigerate until ready for use.

Make the sesame paste by pounding the seeds in a mortar and pestle and then, when crushed, adding the oils and soy sauce—mix well and set to one side.

Make the salsa by combining the mango, lychees, green spring onion, lime juice, roughly chopped coriander leaves, fish sauce and chilli—gently toss. Refrigerate until ready for use.

Brush the fish kebabs with the sesame baste and place onto a medium–hot flat plate. Turn regularly and carefully and baste as you go.

Spoon salsa into the middle of individual plates, top with kebabs and decorate with plenty of coriander leaves.

I try to use stainless steel skewers as they conduct some heat through to the middle of fish pieces so they cook evenly.

BALMAIN BUGS WITH DILL AND LEMON RISOTTO AND BROWNED BUTTER

SERVES 4

8 green bug tails, shell removed

garlic oil spray

400g fava (broad) beans, shelled

1 teaspoon extra virgin olive oil

dill and lemon risotto (see page 160)

100g butter, melted and browned over medium heat, warm

4 lemon cheeks

Make sure the veins are removed from the back of the bug tails. Refrigerate until ready to cook. Boil the fava beans in salted water for 1 minute. Strain and cool under cold water. These can be eaten as they are, but are better with the thick greyish skin removed. This will reveal a brilliant emerald green bean and that is what you want. To remove this skin, pinch the bottom of each bean with your thumb and forefinger and the inner bean will pop out. It is best done as soon as they are cool enough to handle.

Make the dill and lemon risotto and keep warm. This risotto likes being a bit runny, so you may like to add more stock. Spray the tails with oil and seal on hot flat plate; move to medium–hot open grill to cook through and slightly crisp.

Reheat the beans in a microwave with the oil; spoon risotto into the middle of flattish bowls, scatter the beans evenly around the base, top with two bug tails and spoon over some browned butter. Serve with good green salad.

To remove the skin, pinch the bottom of each bean with your thumb and forefinger and the inner bean will pop out.

DILL AND LEMON RISOTTO

30ml olive oil

2 tablespoons onions, finely chopped

1 clove garlic, chopped

1 cup Italian arborio rice

4 cups boiling fish/prawn stock

3 tablespoons dill, chopped

1/2 teaspoon lemon essence

2 tablespoons Parmesan cheese, finely grated

1 teaspoon sea salt

1/2 teaspoon white pepper

Heat oil in a large, heavy-based saucepan over medium heat and fry onions and garlic until soft and golden. Increase heat to high and add the rice—stir for 1 minute.

Add 1 cup boiling stock and cook, stirring, until it is absorbed. Add stock a cupful at a time, stirring constantly, for 15–20 minutes or until rice is tender and all liquid is absorbed.

Stir in dill, lemon essence, cheese, salt and pepper. Cover with lid and leave risotto to sit for 3 minutes before serving. This will make around 550–600g of risotto.

BUG TAILS AND DILL RISOTTO CAKES WITH GARLIC, WHITE WINE AND ANCHOVY CREAM

SERVES 4

8 green Moreton Bay/Balmain Bug tails

spray garlic oil

400g (14oz) basic cooled risotto (see page 166)

3 tablespoons chopped dill

½ teaspoon lemon essence

breadcrumbs

1 cup garlic, white wine and anchovy cream sauce

GARLIC, WHITE WINE ANCHOVY CREAM

2 cloves garlic, crushed

½ cup white wine

450ml pouring cream

1 x 45g can anchovies, drained

1 tablespoon parsley, coarsely chopped

¼ teaspoon cayenne

Cut the bugs in half lengthwise and rinse clean or buy them already split down the middle. Refrigerate until ready to use.

Mix the risotto with the dill and lemon essence. Divide into 8 even amounts and roll into balls with wet hands. Roll in breadcrumbs and flatten slightly to allow for even cooking on the barbecue. Cover and refrigerate for at least 1 hour before use.

Spray the flesh of the bugs with the oil and cook on a medium-hot grill, turning regularly. If you put the flesh side directly onto the grill, make sure it is well oiled.

Cook the risotto cakes on a well-oiled medium-hot plate and cook slowly to allow the heat to penetrate. Turn regularly and allow to brown.

Place all garlic, white wine and anchovy cream ingredients into a saucepan and simmer until the mixture reduces to half the volume.

Serve the bugs on a platter with the cakes on another plate and the heated sauce alongside. A green salad completes this meal.

SPICE-CRUSTED SCALLOPS WITH KUMARA MASH AND MIXED PEA COMPOTE

SERVES 4

16 large scallops, roe on

1 teaspoon caraway seeds

$1/2$ teaspoon white peppercorns

$1/2$ teaspoon sea salt

$1/2$ teaspoon paprika

$1/2$ teaspoon allspice

100g snow peas, trimmed

100g sugar snap peas, trimmed

100g green peas, frozen

1 tablespoon butter

olive oil spray

kumara mash (see page 167)

Trim the scallops of the black membrane and refrigerate until ready for use. Dry roast the caraway seeds and peppercorns for 30 seconds. Tip into a mortar and pestle and when cooled, add the salt and grind to a fine powder. Add the paprika and allspice and mix with the pestle.

Take the scallops from the refrigerator 15 minutes before use. Sprinkle both sides of the scallops liberally with the spice mix and pat it onto each scallop. Spray with oil and cook on a hot flat plate for 30 seconds on each side. If they are very large scallops, you will need to cook for 1 minute but make sure you don't overcook these succulent beauties.

Boil the snow peas and sugar snap peas for 2 minutes in salted water. Add the green peas and bring back to the boil. Cook for 1 minute, strain and toss with butter.

Spoon 4 equal amounts of mash around the perimeter of individual dinner plates. Top with a scallop and spoon the pea compote into the centre.

If you don't like kumara or it is not available you can use mashed potato or white sweet potato, as pictured.

BASIC RISOTTO

30g butter

3 tablespoons onions, finely chopped

2 clove garlic, chopped

1 cup Italian arborio rice

4 cups boiling fish/prawn stock

3 tablespoons parmesan cheese, finely grated

1 teaspoon salt

½ teaspoon white pepper

2 tablespoon dill, finely chopped

Melt butter in a large heavy saucepan and fry onion and garlic until soft and golden. Stir in the rice and cook for 3 minutes, stirring constantly, then add 1 cup boiling stock stirring until it is absorbed. Add stock a cupful at a time and stir constantly, for 15–20 minutes or until rice is tender and all liquid is absorbed—the risotto should be creamy and white.

Stir in cheese, salt, pepper and dill. Cover with lid and leave risotto to sit for 3 minutes before serving.

This will make around 500–600 grams.

KUMARA MASH

300g kumara, peeled and roughly chopped

200g Pontiac potatoes, peeled and roughly chopped

60g onion, finely chopped

1 teaspoon red chilli, finely chopped

4 tablespoons coconut milk, warmed

Boil the kumara and potatoes until well done. Strain and return to saucepan with lid to sit for 3 minutes. Add the onion, chilli and milk and mash to a smoothish paste.

This mash makes very good cakes—you may need to take up excess moisture with a little plain flour. They can be barbecued after they have been breadcrumbed, crusted in polenta or rolled in flour. You should spray them well with oil before cooking.

OCEAN TROUT ON NICOISE SALAD

SERVES 4

4 x 180g ocean trout fillets

olive oil spray

150g Desiree potato slices, 2cm thick and boiled until cooked but firm

3 roma tomatoes, trimmed and cut into wedges

200g green beans, whole, trimmed and blanched

2 hard-boiled eggs, peeled and quartered lengthwise

3 tablespoons extra virgin olive oil

2 tablespoons white wine vinegar

8 anchovy fillets

20 kalamata olives

cracked black pepper to taste

Spray the fillets with a little oil and cook on hot flat plate for 2 minutes. This fish is best cooked medium and the cooking time will depend on the thickness of your fish. Remove and let cool to room temperature.

Heap potatoes, tomatoes, beans and hard-boiled egg quarters into the centre of a flat plate. Scatter the olives around the vegetables and eggs.

Mix the olive oil and vinegar together and spoon over the ingredients on the plate.

Top with ocean trout, sprinkle with black pepper and serve.

BARBECUED GRAVALAX OCEAN TROUT

Serves 4

600g ocean trout fillet skin on

4 teaspoons coarse sea salt

4 teaspooons white sugar

¼ cup fresh dill, finely chopped

4 teaspoons single malt scotch whisky

Spray olive oil

BUTTERED CHATS, PARSLEY AND BLACK PEPPER

400g chats (or small new potatoes)

60g melted butter

2 tablespoons parsley, chopped

½ tablespoon ground black pepper

Trim the ocean trout if necessary.

Mix salt and sugar together and sprinkle onto a large piece of plastic wrap in same shape as trout piece. Spread the dill over the top of this and drizzle over the whisky. Lay trout fillet skin-side up on mix and tightly fold in the cling wrap. Refrigerate skin-side up for 2 hours.

Unwrap, thoroughly brush off dill mix and cut into four pieces. Spray with oil on both sides.

Put the fish, skin-side down, on medium hot plate for 2 minutes or until skin is crisp and brown; turn spray oiled ocean trout over and cooked cured side for ½ minute.

Boil the potatoes in salted boiling water until done. Drain and return to saucepan. Put hood on and let sit for 2 minutes. Add the butter, parsley and pepper and replace the hood. Toss holding the hood on to coat the potatoes.

Serve trout sitting beside the butter-drizzled new potatoes on individual plates and with a green salad.

SEARED OCEAN TROUT ON APPLE, FIG, WALNUT AND CELERY SALAD

SERVES 4

4 x 180g ocean trout
steaks

olive oil spray

sea salt

4 lemon cheeks

apple, fig, walnut and
celery salad (see page
176)

Trim the fish and refrigerate until ready to cook.

Spray skin with a little oil and sprinkle on a little salt. Cook the fish on a hot flat plate skin side down for 1 minute. Lightly spray the flesh side with oil and turn and cook for 2 minutes. If the fish is sliced thin, it will take less time.

Remove and serve on individual dinner plates with the lemon cheeks and salad piled beside the fish.

SPANISH-STYLE SARDINES WITH AIOLI AND CHICKPEA CARROT SALAD

SERVES 4

24 whole sardines

200g baby carrots, peeled and cut on the diagonal

300g canned chickpeas, drained and rinsed

1 teaspoon cinnamon, ground

1 teaspoon cumin, ground

1 large lemon, zest

1 large lemon, juiced

1 small red chilli, deseeded and finely sliced

2 tablespoons honey

½ cup olive oil

sea salt

olive oil spray

aioli (see page 177)

Make sure the sardines are gutted and well cleaned. Refrigerate until ready to cook. Cook the carrots in boiling water for a few minutes or until just tender. Mix the remaining ingredients. Drain the carrots when ready and add to the chickpea mixture. Toss well to combine and leave to cool.

Press some sea salt onto the sardines, spray with oil and cook on medium–hot open grill until done. I do these in batches of 6–8 as they cook quickly. Make sure you place them across the grill as they can fall into the open slats. Cook until done.

Spoon the salad onto the sides of individual dinner plates, pile the sardines besides the salad and spoon a big dollop of aioli beside the sardines and serve immediately.

APPLE, FIG, WALNUT AND CELERY SALAD

2 medium eating apples, cored, halved and cut into half moon slices

2 dried figs, trimmed and cut into thin slices

1 cup celery, diced

1 cup celery leaves, washed and crisped, loosely packed

½ cup walnuts

½ cup mayonnaise

1 tablespoon Indian curry powder

1 tablespoon cider vinegar

Toss the apples, fig slices, celery, celery leaves and walnuts in a salad bowl. Mix the mayonnaise, curry powder and vinegar together then pour over the apple mix and toss well.

It is important to do all this quickly as the apple will quickly brown if allowed to sit without being coated with the dressing.

HUEY'S AIOLI

½ cup good mayonnaise

3 tablespoons sour cream

1 teaspoon Dijon mustard

3 cloves garlic, crushed

1 tablespoon lemon juice

Whisk all the ingredients together for this quick, delicious version of aioli.

Iain Hewitson is one of the world's best chefs who has shown us how to cook and eat well for over three decades. He's a great bloke who adores his food. His influence in the Melbourne restaurant scene—and Australian food at large—is well recognised.

Barney's Bar on Fitzroy Street in Melbourne's St Kilda, is the place to go. This is a recipe he has let me use from Huey's Best Ever Barbecue Recipes.

CUTTLEFISH WITH CHORIZO, CAPSICUM AND PINE NUT SALAD

SERVES 4

400g cuttlefish, body only

¼ cup good olive oil

250g chorizo (hot Spanish sausage), cut into 1cm-thick slices

150g yellow capsicum, deseeded and cut into bite-sized pieces

½ cup pine nuts, toasted

20 grape tomatoes, halved

2 tablespoon zest of lemon, finely grated

¼ cup lemon juice

2 tablespoons Italian parsley, roughly chopped

sea salt to taste

2 tablespoons good olive oil

100g mixed salad leaves

Cut each cuttlefish open to form one large flat piece. Trim and, with a very sharp knife, score the flesh into diamond shapes. Cut into bite-sized pieces and put into a bowl. Pour the first lot of olive oil in and toss the cuttlefish in it—marinate for 15 minutes and if any longer, refrigerate. Put the capsicum, pine nuts and tomato halves into the salad bowl. Mix the lemon zest, juice and salt and pour over the capsicum mix. Add the chopped parsley and toss together—refrigerate until ready for use.

Put the cuttlefish onto a medium–hot flat plate, scored side down—these pieces will curl so you need to move them around to ensure all the surfaces are exposed to the heat. Cuttlefish cooks quickly so do not overcook as it toughens. Remove from the barbecue and put into a bowl. Tip the capsicum mixture over and toss to coat and cool the fish. Let rest.

Put the chorizo slices on the hot open grill. Let them crisp and brown and remove when done.

Pour the second lot of olive oil over the salad leaves and toss, Divide the sausage slices into equal amounts on individual plates, add some salad onto the top of the sausage slices and put pieces of the cuttlefish and capsicum mixture on top and around the salad. Spoon any juices from the cuttlefish over if you like.

SNAPPER FILLETS WITH CHIVE VERJUICE BUTTER AND SALMON ROE

Serves 4

4 x 180g snapper fillets

olive oil spray

24 large green beans, topped and tailed

4 tablespoons salmon roe

CHIVE VERJUICE BUTTER

150g butter, at room temperature

¼ cup chives, chopped

1 tablespoon verjuice

1 teaspoon white pepper, ground

Put the butter, chives, verjuice and pepper into a food processor and pulse until combined. Lift out with a spatula onto a piece of plastic wrap or waxed paper. Shape into a log/roll and freeze to set for at least 30 minute or, better still, longer so the flavours meld.

Trim the fish fillets and check for scales. Pat dry with towelling and spray with oil before cooking on a medium–hot flat plate, starting with flesh side down. Spray the skin side of the fillet and turn after a couple of minutes. The thickness of the fish will determine how long they cook on this side. When you turn each fillet, put the spatula/flipper on top to stop the fillet curling.

Boil the green beans until done—firm but cooked through. Serve the fish on individual plates with the green beans alongside and top with a good thick slice of the chive butter as well as a tablespoon of the roe on top of the butter.

Great with a green salad and sourdough bread.

ALMOND AND PARSLEY-CRUSTED SNAPPER FILLETS

SERVES 4

4 x 180g snapper fillets

¼ cup flat leaf parsley leaves, finely chopped

¼ cup green spring onions, finely chopped

¼ cup almonds, skin on and finely chopped

1 clove garlic, minced

1 tablespoon capers, rinsed

½ cup breadcrumbs, fresh

1 egg white

vegetable oil spray

baking paper

4 lemon wedges

Trim the fish fillets if necessary and refrigerate until ready to cook.

Mix the parsley, spring onions, almonds, garlic, capers and breadcrumbs. Whisk the egg white with a fork and tip half into the crust mixture and tumble to combine well.

Pat the fish dry with paper towelling and brush with remaining half egg white. Spoon and pat a layer of the parsley mix onto each fish fillet. Spray a suitably sized flat baking tray with oil, line with baking paper and spray the paper with oil. Carefully lift the snapper fillets onto the baking tray.

Put a cake cooling rack or similar onto the hot flat plate and sit the fish on that. Cook on a moderately hot barbecue with the lid down for 6–8 minutes—time depends on the thickness of the fish fillet.

Remove and serve with a lemon wedge to one side and a good big bowl of a mixed green leaf salad.

For this fish dish I suggest you use the thinner tail end of the snapper fillets.

SNAPPER FILLETS WITH CANNELLINI BEAN AND ESCHALOT SALAD

SERVES 4

4 x 180g snapper fillets

400g canned cannellini beans, drained

2 large eschalots, finely chopped

¼ cup semi roasted tomatoes, roughly chopped

1 tablespoon parsley, roughly chopped

½ cup olive oil

1 tablespoon prepared Dijon mustard paste

¼ cup cider vinegar

sea salt and ground black pepper to taste

olive oil spray

4 lime halves

Trim the fish, if necessary, and refrigerate until ready to use.

Make the salad by tumbling the beans, eschalots, tomatoes and parsley together. Whisk the oil and mustard together. Dribble in the vinegar while whisking. Season with salt and ground black pepper to taste and spoon over the bean mix. Mix well and let sit for 2 hours, refrigerated, before serving.

Spray the fish with oil and cook on medium–hot flat plate until done. Cook the lime halves, cut side down, on a very hot open grill to lightly brown and mark the cut flesh.

To serve, spoon the bean salad into the centre of individual flattish bowls, top with the snapper and put the limes beside the fish with the cooked flesh side up.

SKEWERED TIKKA-INFUSED SNAPPER WITH CUCUMBER AND MINT DIP

SERVES 4

600g snapper fillets, cut into bite-sized pieces

4–8 stainless steel skewers

1 cup natural yoghurt

1 tablespoon cider vinegar

2 tablespoons tikka paste

1 tablespoon mint

4–8 lime cheeks

CUCUMBER AND MINT DIP

1 cup natural yoghurt

¼ cup cucumber flesh, finely diced

2 tablespoons mint, finely shredded

Mix cucumber and mint ingredients well at least 4 hours before use, and refrigerate.

Thread equal numbers of snapper pieces onto the skewers. Mix the yoghurt, vinegar, tikka paste and mint together.

On a large, flat glass dish, spoon the tikka mixture over the fish skewers and let them sit in the marinade for at least 30 minutes. Turn every 10 minutes or spoon the marinade over them.

Cook on a medium–hot flat plates until done. Turn regularly and brush with the tikka mixture as you go. These will take around 10 minutes to cook and they go quite crusty as they do.

Serve snapper on a platter, with the lime cheeks, in the middle of the table with a bowl of the dipping sauce beside the fish. A good green salad and some heated pita bread or naan completes this dish.

CALAMARI WITH LIME JUICE AND CORIANDER

SERVES 4

6 medium calamari tubes, cleaned

3 fresh tablespoons lime juice

1 tablespoon peanut oil

1 small red chilli, deseeded and minced

1 root coriander, washed and minced

3 teaspoons fish sauce (nam pla)

1 teaspoon palm sugar

spray oil

sprigs of coriander, washed and crisped in refrigerator

Slit the tubes down one side and open to lay flat, skin side down, and score finely. Cut into bite- sized pieces.

Make a marinade by combining the lime juice, peanut oil, chilli, coriander root, fish sauce and sugar. Mix well. Soak the scored calamari in this marinade for 15 minutes.

Lift the calamari from the marinade and drain off any excess juices.

Spray a hot plate with oil and put the calamari onto it. Cook in small batches.

Tumble and turn the pieces, cooking for no longer than 2 minutes.

Decorate with scattered torn coriander leaves and serve.

INDEX